KARATE:

BENEATH THE SURFACE

Copyright 2017, Kamen Entertainment Group, Inc.

All rights reserved. Copyright under Berne Copyright Convention, Universal Copyright Convention, and Pan-American Copyright Convention. No part of this book may be reproduced, stored in a retrieval system, or transmitted in any form, or by any means, electronic, mechanical, photocopying, recording or otherwise, anywhere in the universe, in perpetuity without prior permission of the author.

Published by: Kamen Entertainment Group, Inc. 2017
New York, NY USA

ISBN-13: 978-0-9990427-0-0
ISBN-10: 0-9990427-0-X

Forward by: Marina Kamen
Edited by: Justin Bartholemew Kamen, Esq. and Philip Weissman
Additional Editing by: Melvin Isidore Morgenstein Ed.D.
Consultant: Robert Mark Kamen, Ph.D.
Proofreading: Tess Molly Kamen and Elinore Kamen
Graphic Design by: Tyler Michael Kamen
Cover art by: Erika Pochybova and James W. Johnson

KARATE:

BENEATH THE SURFACE

BY ROY KENNETH KAMEN

Published by:

Kamen Entertainment Group, Inc.

2017

First Edition

Dedication

I dedicate this book to those who have

gone before

and transmitted their knowledge

faithfully and fully.

I bow and say:

*"**Please Teach Me**"*

Foreword

By: Marina Kamen

I met my husband Roy Kenneth Kamen in 1982.

The 80s! A time when "yuppies" represented the young people in their 20s and 30s who were first coming into their own. A time to party while watching MTV, drink fine wine and have money finally flow again after a decade of one of the worst recessions in American history. While most young men at this stage of life were busy chasing that "golden ticket", Roy was different.

He was working as a recording engineer in NYC and going home every night to his house in Queens, NY, which he shared with his friend and fellow Martial Arts enthusiast Philip Weissman. It is in this house that these men converted a 30-foot basement into a Dojo for young people to learn the Martial Art style of GoJu-Ryu. Roy and Philip taught lessons to a group of teens that also taught back by sharing their lives, passions, emotions and desires for learning this Martial Art.

In 1984, Roy's eldest brother wrote and hit the world with the film "The Karate Kid". We all remember watching the emotional connection between a young boy Daniel and his teacher Mr. Miyagi in this coming of age classic. This film was able to weave a thread of emotion and fearless compassion between student, teacher and an art form that presented a circle of life approach touching millions of heart strings like a well tuned orchestra of movement and growth.

So here is the question: What is the connection of mind, body, spirit, fearlessness and compassion?

As you read this book many other questions regarding the Martial Arts, and in particular the GoJu-Ryu style, will ignite inquisitive light bulbs in your own minds. Most of us think of Karate or the Martial Arts as a way to fight, defend ourselves or just get a bit of exercise. In these following pages, Roy explores a deeper purpose of the connective definition of the words "mind, body and spirit" and may leave you with the question of why the martial arts are referred to as an "art form" in the first place.

Preface

This book is for Martial Artists who train their bodies and minds, but have yet to find the spirit that lies *deep* within their art.

Martial Arts are brutal and deadly forms of fighting, but they also contain the potential to go beyond the surface of skin and bones defensive and aggressive physical techniques by tapping into a well of emotional and spiritual energy that strengthens the physical motion, while elevating character and personal growth.

What you are about to read may alter how you view and practice Martial Arts. I offer the reader an alternative to commonly held beliefs about the Martial Arts and Okinawan GoJu-Ryu Kata, specifically.

The revelations I have had were not taught by any of my teachers, tutors or mentors. While these learned and skilled people may have planted signposts along the way for my discoveries, they have not officially taught the final conclusions to me in or out of the Dojo. These ideas about the nature of Karate and Kata are mine, and mine alone.

While focused on GoJu-Ryu Karate Kata, these ideas can be applied to any Martial Art. You just have to know what to look for.

This is my path, my journey and my discoveries of what lies beneath the surface of the art I have held in my heart for over 40 years.

Acknowledgements

There are so many people I'd like to thank on the path to writing this book. My wife and life partner Marina Kamen, who taught me how motion and emotions are linked, who helped guide me through life to "feel" and who always supported me. My eldest brother and first Karate teacher, Robert Mark Kamen, who introduced me to the world of Martial Arts, always with a good dose of reality and whom I consider my father in the Martial Arts. Terry Kamen, my older brother, who laid the foundation for my journey to higher consciousness; I see myself in your eyes Terry. My Shotokan teacher Toyotaro Miyazaki, who taught me to never criticize another man's technique but to watch closely and steal it. My first GoJu instructor, who taught me that people are sometimes not what they appear to be. My current Karate tutor and dear friend Kow Loon Ong (Kayo), who "took me in", taught me how deep the rabbit hole goes in the Martial Arts and allowed me the freedom to explore and develop my own way. Martial Artist, world explorer and published author, Gary Gabelhouse, who opened my eyes to the concepts of Kata as Mudra, Mantra and Mandala. David Wong, another of my mentors and historian of Chinese history, culture and Martial Arts. Kayo's family Lai, John, Max and Pearl Ong, and Chi-I-Do members Christopher Chin, Howard Lau, Kevin Lau, Jonathan Reingold, Matthew Simmons and Bai Zhou Zhu for their deep and supportive friendship and guidance. My parents, Elinore and Harry, who gave me life and instilled in me strong values. To my children who put everything in my life into perspective. Additional kudos to Justin Bartholemew Kamen and Philip Weissman for their editing prowess, Tess Molly Kamen and Elinore Kamen for their proofreading skills and Tyler Michael Kamen who helped me graphically design this book. Thank you to Donna Rockwell Psy.D. who helped me be more mindful and coaxed me to start putting my thoughts down on paper. And lastly, thank you very much to all of my fellow Chi-I-Do students and fellow Budo brother followers of "The Way".

Special thanks to Erika Pochybova and James W. Johnson for the beautiful cover art entitled "Twilight", which captures the essence of this book and all the beauty that lies "beneath the surface".

KARATE:
BENEATH THE SURFACE

BY ROY KENNETH KAMEN

Table of Contents

DEDICATION V

FOREWORD VII

PREFACE VIII

ACKNOWLEDGEMENTS IX

INTRODUCTION 1

CHAPTER 1: *PERSPECTIVE* 5
    THREE MARTIAL ARTS OF CHINA 7
    CHINESE MARTIAL ARTS COME TO OKINAWA 8
    KANRYO HIGASHIONNA 9
    CHOJUN (TYAJUN) MIYAGI 10
    THE BIRTH OF GOJU-RYU KARATE 11
    SEIKO HIGA 12
    SEIKICHI TOGUCHI 13
    THE BROKEN HEART 14
    KARATE COMES TO AMERICA 15
    KARATE TODAY 16

CHAPTER 2: *MY BEGINNINGS* 17
    PLANTING SEEDS 19
    THE CIRCLE OF SHOES 20
    TROUBLESHOOTING 21
    MY JOURNEY 22
    KAYO KILLED MY KARATE 26
    KOW LOON ONG 28
    LEAVING SHOREI-KAN 29
    BESHERT 30
    FIX IT IN THE MIX 32

CHAPTER 3: *CULTIVATING THE WAY* 33
    PATHS TO ENLIGHTENMENT 35
    MY DOJO 36
    SACRED SPACE 37
    MIRRORS 37
    AMBIGUITY 38

Alone In A Crowd	39
Martial Virtues	39
Integrity	41
Trust	43
Mindset	44
Chi	44
Breathing	45
Breath As Spiritual Matter	46
Kiai	48
The Yin and Yang of Technique	49
Repetition, Persistence and Patience	50
Mushin	51
Imagination	52

CHAPTER 4: *CHANGE* 53

Growing Old	55
Thinking Outside The Box	56
San Lorenzo Dojo	56
The Great Oak Tree Sensei	59
Shu Ha Ri and Mochi Bun	60
The Go and the Ju in GoJu	62
Music and Kata	63
The Art of the Martial Arts	64
A New Perspective	66
Mudra, Mantra and Mandala	67

CHAPTER 5: *PREPARING THE GROUND* 69

What Is Kata	71
Kata Names	73
Kata By The Numbers	75
Kata and the Five Elements	76
Kata and the Animals	78
Kata Fighting Applications	79
Kata As An Emotional State	79
Cracking Open with Kururunfa	81
Upward Hands Raised in Prayer	82
Stepping Stones	84

CHAPTER 6: *KATA* 85
- OPENING KATA 87
- CLOSING KATA 88
- THE MANDALAS OF KATA 89
- SANCHIN 90
- TENSHO 92
- SAIFA 94
- SEIYUNCHIN 96
- SEISAN 98
- SEIPAI 100
- SHISOCHIN 102
- SANSEIRU 104
- KURURUNFA 106
- PEICHURIN 108
- APPLYING EMOTION IN KATA 110

CHAPTER 7: *COMPASSION* 111
- THINGS ARE THE WAY THEY ARE 113
- THE KILLER MONKS OF SHAOLIN 114
- FEARLESS COMPASSION 115
- WHAT DOES COMPASSION LOOK LIKE 116
- PERSONAL COMPASSION 117
- BETRAYAL 118
- ABUSE 118
- MARTIAL ARTS VS. MARITAL ARTS 120

CHAPTER 8: *THE PEACE WITHIN* 121
- BALANCING THE TRIAD OF LIFE 123
- HEALING 123
- LOVE WHAT YOU DO 124
- FORGIVENESS 125
- LIVING IN THE JU 126
- FACING YOUR WORST ENEMY 127

EPILOGUE 129

APPENDIX 131

Introduction

> ### *A Path To Enlightenment.*
>
> *The Kata of Traditional Okinawan GoJu-Ryu Karate hold a secret.*
>
> *By passing through the various Kata of the system, a student gradually progresses through physical, emotional and spiritual states that ultimately provide a roadmap to becoming a fearless and compassionate human being.*

I always believed that by studying the Martial Arts, I could break through my personal limitations and become a fully realized person. I was fortunate to discover a man who had a traditional, yet somewhat eccentric method of teaching and way of being. And a year after meeting this man, fortune once again touched me when my wife Marina walked into my life. Together, they helped foster the feelings that stir inside of me today, that inspired me to write this book.

I have practiced Okinawan GoJu-Ryu Karate since 1974, attending classes several times a week. However, I have taken several "breaks" from the Dojo. My first break occurred after learning Sanseiru Kata, a Kata of "projection". Kow Loon Ong, known to his students as "Kayo", has been my tutor and friend since 1981. He taught traditional Okinawan GoJu-Ryu Karate as a deadly fighting art. Karate's purpose was not exercise or spiritual development; its was for brutal combat.

Karate: Beneath The Surface

I started imagining fights in every location I found myself in and soon realized that I would be attracting the very thing I did not want... to fight. Out of this fear, I stopped training at the Dojo for a couple of years.

During that time, I continued to research the Martial Arts and practice at home. I came to understand that in order to reach the highest spiritual level through Karate, the techniques in Kata *must* be brutal and deadly. I understood that the masters of old who created this art did so after surviving many life or death encounters and therefore developed their art to be deadly. Only then could they attain the "enlightenment" that I was seeking.

So, I went back to the Dojo and rededicated myself to training and fill the void in my knowledge.

Throughout this time Marina, a professional director, producer and performer, enabled me to get in touch with my emotions, something I always had trouble expressing. The merger of the physical art with free flowing, yet controlled emotions, took my understanding of the Martial Arts to a new level.

Then, one beautiful summer day, it all came together. I experienced a profound spiritual realization, connecting the past to the present and giving me further insight into the purpose of the art I had been studying for over 40 years.

This book is my way of passing on the lessons learned during my journey to understand the "spiritual" side of the art and to use them to impact my life in a positive way.

Many of the ideas set forth herein may be hard to grasp for the many Martial Artists who have been raised "in the box" that Karate is a physical fighting art and nothing more.

My hopes are that a few will follow my path and find a deeper meaning in Kata and, therefore, in life.

INTRODUCTION

My art is traditional Okinawan GoJu-Ryu Karate, a half hard, half soft style. The commonly held understanding is that in GoJu-Ryu we strike hard with strong and direct attacks (*Go* means "hard" in Japanese), while we block softly with circular and deflective movements (*Ju* means "soft"). I have come, however, to understand an alternative view that the "hard" of GoJu-Ryu is everything physical; that which we can touch and see, including all movements of the body. The Ju, or soft side of the art, is all the stuff we cannot see, or touch. It is the emotional and spiritual side; the part of the art that few acknowledge, understand or train to develop. Without this Ju or soft side, Karate is only one half an art form.

Most traditional Martial Arts schools contain Kata as part of their curriculum. A Kata is a dance-like pattern of fighting techniques containing specific hand and foot positions and movements, specific breathing patterns, vocalizations, and visualization of imaginary opponents. Physical, emotional and spiritual energies are generated, absorbed, redirected and projected. Kata is essentially a combat-based energy management system. Throughout a GoJu-Ryu Kata, many hard and soft techniques are incorporated.

There are three types of GoJu-Ryu Kata; Bible Kata, Hookyu Kata (Training Kata), and Koryu Kata (Classical Kata). Students learn the Kata in a systematic approach where each progressing Kata is more difficult than the previous one. It takes many years to master all of the intricate movements and fighting strategies contained in the Kata.

So how does this lead down a path to enlightenment?

The Bible and Koryu Kata of GoJu-Ryu Karate hold the secret. These Kata have ancient roots containing advanced fighting techniques, fighting strategies *and* deep spiritual meaning. By passing through the various Kata of the system, a student gradually progresses through physical, emotional and spiritual states that ultimately provide a roadmap to becoming a fearless and compassionate human being; a person who can give freely, because he *can* fight and is not afraid of losing anything, including his life.

Karate: Beneath The Surface

The rigorous training Martial Artists suffer through, as we learn to fight by mastering the Kata, elevates our character as we overcome our physical, emotional and spiritual limitations. The lessons we learn through training increase our compassion as we teach our juniors, whom are themselves suffering through the training.

> *"Respect your seniors and treat your juniors kindly."*
> ~ Master Seikichi Toguchi

We become sensitive to the suffering we, and all around us have experienced and endured. Many people's problems stem from abuse, in which suffering is rooted. Those who wish us harm do so as a result of abuse they have endured sometime in their life. We see the results of abuse all around us. Children, spouses, friends and colleagues are all potential victims of abuse. The far-reaching effects of abuse destroy lives and interfere with the natural harmony of life. Compassion is the antidote for the suffering caused by abuse. By embracing and extending compassion we can end our own and others suffering, and make a positive difference in the world.

This is the promise and final end-goal of traditional Martial Arts and Okinawan GoJu-Ryu Karate, and is sadly missing in the arts as practiced today.

The purpose of studying Karate is not to learn how to fight.

Fighting is only a means to an end.

The purpose is to become compassionate.

You must be fearless to be truly compassionate.

It is a path to enlightenment.

Chapter 1: *Perspective*

Before jumping into the deep water, I feel it's important to put things into historical perspective.

Where did our Martial Arts come from? What were the influences that caused the art to evolve into what it is today? What has been gained or lost through generations of hands-on transmission, cultural influences and political meddling?

The seeds of Okinawan GoJu-Ryu Karate originally came from India many centuries ago in the form of religion, dance, meditation and warfare. These separate yet connected practices coalesced to become the Martial Arts of China.

From China, the Martial Arts were exported to the island of Okinawa and then exploded worldwide into what is known today as Karate.

Chapter 1: *Perspective*

Three Martial Arts of China

There were three Martial Arts in China, one with a military history, one with a family history and one with a spiritual history. In many cases, the three have combined in various formulations to create many different styles. Most are quite effective and deadly. These Martial Arts (Kung Fu) were exported from China to Okinawa, mixed with the indigenous Martial Art of "Te" (hand) and became known as Karate. It is my thought that only one of these three Martial Arts is practiced today, the others being mostly lost to the passage of time and the teacher's lack of understanding that was passed down to his students. There are still pockets around the world that practice with the spiritual and family lineage as part of their system but they are few and far between. They are considered "the old way".

The three popular stories about the origin of Karate are as follows:

• **Military** - In China, for thousands of years, provinces fought each other for land and resources. Each province built an army and each man was taught how to fight with and without weapons. During peacetime when the Government was executing renegade soldiers who had become either bandits or revolutionaries, the Shaolin Temple became a refuge. Over time, the fighting methods evolved and were exported to Okinawa and other nations throughout the East. This is the Karate that is widely known and practiced in Dojos all over the world. It is brutal and focuses exclusively on fighting and self-defense. In recent years, this approach evolved into tournament Karate, a shadow of its former purpose, eliminating all of the maiming and killing techniques.

• **Family or Village Style** - Martial Arts was practiced in small villages all over China often being passed on from father to son. The knowledge was kept hidden from the general public. This was known as Family or Village Style Martial Arts. The origin of these systems is shrouded in mystery. Most likely the father of the family learned the art from his father, in the military, at Shaolin, from a teacher from those sources or from another family style in another village.

Many of these family styles died out in 1966 during the Cultural Revolution when China's leader Mao Zedong enforced communism in the country by removing capitalist, traditional and cultural elements from Chinese society, and imposed Maoist orthodoxy.

• **The Shaolin Temple** - Bodhidharma, an Indian Yogi, traveled to China and found the monks in the Shaolin temple in poor physical shape, unable to perform the rigorous meditations and prayer rituals he brought with him from India. He taught the temple's Buddhist monks a system of exercises to strengthen their minds and bodies based on the study of the Sutras (Buddhist texts). The temple was also a refuge for criminals and revolutionaries, who brought their Martial Arts with them. In addition, in keeping with the harmony of nature, the monks observed animals fighting and adopted their fighting styles. This melting pot of religion, military and nature provided the ingredients which became the Martial Arts of Shaolin.

Chinese Martial Arts Come To Okinawa

For centuries, Okinawa traded with China and there was a great deal of back and forth travel. As the people from these two populations mixed, Chinese culture brought by sailors, merchants, government officials and their military escorts heavily influenced Okinawan culture. Along with them came Chinese Martial Arts, which the Okinawans mixed with their own indigenous fighting methods to become the art of To-Te, meaning "Chinese Hand".

There were three main trading centers on Okinawa: Naha, Shuri and Tomari. Each had its own version of To-Te. Naha had Naha-Te (hand of Naha), Shuri has Shuri-Te (hand of Shuri), and Tomari had Tomari-Te (hand of Tomari).

Shuri-Te evolved to become Shorin-Ryu and all its offshoots. Naha-Te, through Master Kanryo Higashionna, evolved to become GoJu-Ryu and all its offshoots. Sadly, Tomari-Te has mostly been lost to time.

The following is a brief history of the lineage of Naha-Te and its offspring, traditional Okinawan GoJu-Ryu Karate.

CHAPTER 1: *PERSPECTIVE*

Kanryo Higashionna

(1853 – 1915)

Kanryo Higashionna, a Naha-Te master, traveled to Fukien Province of southern China and learned a form of Fukien White Crane from a Kung Fu master named Ryu Ryu Ko. Powerful short-range movements, quick long-range movements, circular motions, and synchronization of breath and motion characterized the White Crane system.

For centuries, the Chinese had understood the balance of opposing forces balancing and blending into each other, with a little of each contained in the other. This concept, Yin / Yang, was an underlying principle of Chinese culture and therefore the Martial Arts.

Yin / Yang became a very important characteristic of Higashionna's style in the form of hard and soft properties. Higashionna combined what he learned in China with his Naha-Te art to create a new style which had yet to be named.

Higashionna was known for lightning fast hands and feet. He unfortunately passed his new art onto just a few men on Okinawa.

Chojun (Tyajun) Miyagi
(1888 – 1953)

One of Higashionna's senior students was Chojun Miyagi. Miyagi was a powerful man with a strong body and a vice-like grip. Miyagi devoted his life to the study and further development of his teacher's art. Another student of Higashionna was Seiko Higa. Higa was a junior to Miyagi under Higashionna and trained for several years alongside Miyagi.

After Higashionna's death in 1915, Miyagi traveled back to Fukien Province in search of any information he could find about the origins of his teacher's teacher and his original art. Sadly, he did not find what he was looking for. However, during his travels he was exposed to at least two of the three main Chinese Martial Arts of the Wudang school: The Taoist arts of Bagua Zhang (the Eight Trigram Palm System) and Xing-Yi Quan (Mind Boxing System). Miyagi began incorporating these other systems' concepts into Higashionna's Naha-Te. He made additional trips to China, amassing a unique and large library of books and other written materials on the Chinese and Okinawan Martial Arts. Chojun Miyagi passed away in 1953, coincidentally the same year I was born.

CHAPTER 1: *PERSPECTIVE*

The Birth of GoJu-Ryu Karate

In 1929, there was a meeting in Kyoto Japan, for the All Japan Martial Arts Demonstration. Miyagi sent his senior student Jin'an Shinsato to represent his new art. When asked for the name of this new art, Shinsato off the top of his head called it the "Half Hard - Half Soft" style.

Upon Shinsato's return to Okinawa, Miyagi took this idea and coined the name GoJu based on the poem: "The Eight Laws Of The Fist" from a book called the Bubishi. The poem's line reads: "All the Universe inhales soft (Ju) and exhales hard (Go)."

Go means "hard" as in punch, kick and block with great strength. *Ju* means "soft", as in circular, deflecting blocks and using the opponent's energy against him. Another less popular concept is one of "giving" and "receiving" energy. An attack is considered giving energy (Go) and a block is considered receiving energy (Ju). "Ryu" is short for the Ryukyu Islands, of which Okinawa is the largest.

Miyagi spent the rest of his lifetime fine-tuning his new art of GoJu-Ryu and creating a teaching system whereby the art could be taught in public schools on Okinawa and ultimately around the world.

These must have been exciting times on the small island of Okinawa however, as Japan prepared for World War II and the invasion of China, all things Chinese in Okinawa were Japanized, including the Okinawan Martial Arts, which had their roots in China. As a result, the name To-Te (Chinese hand) was changed to Kara-Te (empty hand).

Seiko Higa
(1898 – 1966)

Seiko Higa is not well known in the modern Martial Arts world. Higa was a junior student in Higashionna's school under Chojun Miyagi. After Higashionna's death, Higa continued his studies under Miyagi and was present as GoJu-Ryu came into being. Higa had a unique opportunity to see how his teacher's original art of Naha-Te was changed into the new art of GoJu-Ryu.

Higa was the only person Miyagi had authorized to teach his new art. While following Miyagi's new GoJu-Ryu system, Higa maintained some of Higashionna's original art and passed this onto his students. Higa's lineage is unique in the GoJu world. His students seem to be *softer and more fluid* than the other mainstream GoJu schools and their offshoots. The Kata of Higa's lineage seem to have more of a *Chinese* flavor.

In my humble opinion, this is due to Higa's resistance to Miyagi's changing Higashionna's art, therefore maintaining some of the original Chinese influence that has brought me to where I am today.

CHAPTER 1: *PERSPECTIVE*

Seikichi Toguchi

(1917 – 1998)

One of Higa's students in Miyagi's Dojo was Seikichi Toguchi, who would later found Shorei-Kan (House of Courtesy and Manners) and become my Grand Master. Toguchi continued the work started by Miyagi and completed the GoJu-Ryu system containing the Taisho Daruma Warm Up, Preparatory Exercises, two Bible Kata, ten Training Kata and associated Bunkai (two man forms), eight Koryu Kata with associated Bunkai, and two man training exercises named Kiso Kumite, Jissen Kumite and Ippon Kumite. He also incorporated classical Okinawan weapons into his system from his good friend Shinpo Matayoshi, one of Okinawa's top weapons men and Master of his family's Kingai-ryu (Golden Rooster) system of Martial Arts. Under the influence of Higa and Matayoshi, Toguchi seemed to have maintained some of the spiritual aspects of the original art and incorporated them into his curriculum.

Following Miyagi's death, Toguchi opened his own Dojo and allowed the post-war occupying American soldiers to join. The US Military paid for the soldier's classes and many Okinawa Karate teachers were able to make a living teaching the American servicemen.

The Broken Heart

Centuries of tradition of passing on the emotional and spiritual sides of the Martial Arts directly from teacher to student in China were broken by The Boxer Rebellion and later Mao Zedong's Cultural Revolution from 1966 – 1976. Religion was purged from society, and that included the teaching of spirit in the Martial Arts. Teachers who did not accept the new government requirements for teaching the Martial Arts were persecuted and even executed. The newly developed Chinese National Martial Art, Wushu, was the only Martial Art allowed under the Communist regime. All religious and spiritual aspects were eliminated from the training.

Luckily long before the turmoil in China many teachers had exported Chinese Martial Arts *in their entirety* to various countries including the island of Okinawa where Chojun Miyagi developed his new art of GoJu-Ryu.

Toward the end of World War II Okinawa was devastated by the American campaign to dislodge the Japanese troops. Between 40,000 to 150,000 Okinawans perished during the battle. Virtually everyone on Okinawa lost relatives, friends and most of their belongings due to the intense bombing and ground combat.

Chojun Miyagi lost family members, friends, students (including his senior-most student Jin'an Shinsato) and his cherished Martial Arts library. Some say he died of a broken heart. I believe the heart of Karate was broken as well.

Karate had become emotionally numb.

Following Miyagi's death, Karate took on a new purpose – tournament competition. This was never the original intent of the Martial Arts. The spiritual and emotional aspects of the art were lost over the years of turmoil. Karate had its heart broken, and today we are left with spiritually empty, unemotional Kata – like abandoned buildings that were once thriving with life. This is surely not the art our ancestors developed, practiced and passed on.

Chapter 1: *Perspective*

Karate Comes To America

Karate was introduced to America by the GI's returning from World War II who discovered Karate in Okinawa and trained there for several years. However, in the few years they studied, they learned only the basics of the art: Blocking, punching and kicking. Therefore the amount of training time spent is important in understanding how limited and rudimentary the art was that they had brought back to America.

In addition, there was great animosity held by the Okinawans toward the Americans who had done so much damage to the island and brought so much hurt and sadness due to the loss of family and friends through the brutal bombing and ground campaign to defeat Japan. It is no wonder that these men did not train in the higher spiritual aspects of the art, since it was generally withheld. In the end, Karate in America was considered an effective deadly fighting art, a competitive sport and nothing more.

In the mid 1960's the Okinawans changed the GoJu-Ryu Kata, simplifying them for worldwide dissemination. As with the Chinese Martial Arts, GoJu-Ryu from before the change is also considered to be "the old way".

In the years since, many Okinawans have visited the United States and traveled around the world spreading the deeper aspects of the art, and many who studied from the American pioneers have returned to Okinawa to learn directly from the source.

A high level Okinawan who visited the United States was Akira Kawakami, one of Toguchi's "3 shining stars" from his first generation of students, the other two being Shinjo Masenobu and Katsuyoshi Kanai. Kawakami also had additional training directly from Higa as well as several other of Miyagi's direct first generation disciples including Dai Sensei Yagi, Miyagi's most senior student.

Kawakami settled in New York City at Thomas Boddie's Shorei-Kan Uptown Dojo where he became Kayo's teacher of "the old way" GoJu-Ryu. Another of Okinawa's top Martial Artists to visit New York City was Shinpo Matayoshi who alongside Toguchi directly trained Kayo in the early 1970's.

Karate Today

It is important to understand one-on-one, hands-on transmission from teacher to student to understand why Karate is what it is today.

Questions arise: How long did the teacher study from his teacher? How much did the teacher really know and how well could he *express* the art? How willing was the teacher and how well could he transmit his knowledge? Did the teacher have bad habits, idiosyncrasies, or physical limitations which his student picked up and became the *new normal* for the style? Was making money the driving factor in the transmission thereby diluting the difficulty and complexity of the art? How did the teacher adapt to the changing social and economic environments, such as insurance, legal and political pressures? Also, we must take into account the student's personal motivation.

This is why there is so much variation from one Dojo to another and even differences within one style.

And today there are different reason for studying Karate besides learning how to fight. Each is quite valid and many practice for multiple reasons. The most common ones for studying the art today are for physical fitness, self-defense and tournament competition. Martial Arts require a strong and flexible body with good cardio endurance.

Then there are the few who approach the art for character elevation and spiritual development. They refer to Kata as "moving meditation" and strive to reach a higher consciousness through the art.

Many children are enrolled in Martial Arts classes by their parents hoping their children will gain some control of their emotions and help them to not "act out" in destructive ways. I find it interesting that virtually no adults choose the Martial Arts for this reason. People I meet everyday could benefit from having more control over their volatile and often destructive emotions.

Chapter 2: *My Beginnings*

All ideas sprout like small seeds planted in fertile soil. With care and nurturing, great forests can grow from just one seed.

Like new buds of Spring on a tree, my life has been a series of new beginnings. Each experience leading to new lessons learned.

As great storms test the strength of a tree, so have the winds of time tested my mettle allowing me to see the world in ways I would never have imagined years ago.

This is my journey, my story, and how it all began.

CHAPTER 2: *My Beginnings*

Planting Seeds

My grandparents came to America before World War I when America held great promise and safety. They struggled to learn the language, and provide for their children. They also followed Jewish traditions, rituals, and life philosophies with which they were raised and they passed them on to their children.

My parents were brought up during the Great Depression. Growing up, I often heard stories about their childhood neighbors who were evicted from their apartments because they couldn't pay the rent. Stories like Morty the peddler with his four children sitting on their sofa in the middle of the street not knowing where to go or where their next meal would come from. Poverty fostered a feeling of community where each family helped the other. Doors were always open and company welcomed. No one complained about not having money or things. They were just happy to have the basics of life and to be alive with the people they loved.

After my father returned from serving in World War II, my parents married and started a family. They moved to the Projects on White Plains Road and Allerton Avenue in the Bronx. Rent was $78 a month. My Dad was an accountant and my Mom stayed home to raise my brothers and me. We lived in a two bedroom, one bathroom apartment, where I shared a bedroom with my two older brothers. It was tight but we didn't know any different, which wouldn't have made a difference anyway since we were taught not to complain. Jewish traditions and close family ties were the centerpiece of our home and life.

My mother rarely expressed her emotions. She had been taught by her parents to watch what words came out of her mouth since "once they were said, they didn't belong to her anymore and she could never take them back". I was the youngest of three children and didn't begin talking until I was about three. I remember not being able to get a word in with my parents and two older brothers ratchet-jawing away.

Besides, what did I have to say as a three year old that was as important as what my elders were talking about? I learned that it was safer to remain silent and keep my thoughts and emotions to myself.

One of my first emotional memories of anger was towards my Mother. I don't remember the exact reason but I felt I couldn't voice my displeasure and took revenge by urinating in the corner of the bathroom next to the toilet. I got her back alright; she had to clean up that mess. I became a passive-aggressive in training. I asked her about that one day recently and she said she never knew about it. So much for not getting a message across. The bottling up of my emotions carried through my childhood well into adulthood.

The Circle Of Shoes

When I was a toddler, for entertainment, my brother Robert, would take all of our shoes, make a circle out of them and put me in the middle. He then told Terry, my middle brother, that if I got out of the circle, Robert would beat *him* up. It was a long time ago and my memories of being the victim in Robert's game are hazy, but, thinking back, I see now that a result of my brother's abusiveness was a passivity that stayed with me for decades; and so, when I found myself in a difficult or seemingly inextricable situation, I accepted my circumstances. Hence, my forty-two years studying just one Martial Art, my thirty-eight year career, and my thirty-four year marriage to one woman. I became an expert in endurance and making things work out.

CHAPTER 2: *My Beginnings*

I have worked hard over the past few years with the guidance of professionals to come to terms with this and to break out of that "circle of shoes". My efforts have enabled me to see past boundaries, which altered my Martial Arts practice. I no longer feel bound by "commonly" held beliefs about GoJu-Ryu Karate. And practicing Kata has been a catalyst for many of these changes.

Troubleshooting

Growing up, I attended a summer camp near Albany, New York. It was a simple camp that didn't cost much to attend. I worked in, then managed, the theater that was housed in an old Dutch barn. We put on a new show every Saturday night. We didn't have much in the way of supplies so I needed to improvise most of the time. Props, lighting, sound; I had to come up with many creative solutions with the few tools at hand. No one understood how I always came up with these ingenious solutions. They just sat back and enjoyed the performances.

I have always been good at troubleshooting. Show me a problem and I can usually find a solution. Just like at camp and through my years in business I noticed that many people don't plan for problems they encounter. They become paralyzed by indecision. Then along comes someone who fixes the problem and the person, who was stuck just a moment ago, moves forward again. I have also noticed that many people don't appreciate the help of others because it highlights their own incompetence.

Jealousy comes in all forms.

I have experienced jealousy from others as I solved problems when they made mistakes.

In Karate, Kata are like puzzles with clues that need to be examined and deciphered. They are like knots that need to be *untied* if they are to be mastered.

Troubleshooting and problem solving are necessary skills in Martial Arts to understand what the Kata movements mean.

My Journey

I began my Karate journey at thirteen years old. My brother Robert was my first Sensei (meaning, one who has gone before or teacher).

Robert's introduction to the Martial Arts was due to an event at the 1964 World's Fair in Flushing Queens, NYC. While he was enjoying the exhibitions, Robert was targeted and chased by a gang out for Jewish blood. Being on the High School track team, he was able to outrun the gang and he found himself outside of Ed McGrath's "American Dojo" in Queens NY (Dojo meaning place to learn "The Way"), teaching an Okinawan style of Karate known as Isshin-Ryu. It happened to be one of the toughest Dojos in the country, winning many of the full contact tournaments held in the 1960's. Robert joined the Dojo and his path was set.

Years passed. Robert used me and my brother Terry as his practice dummies, earned his Black Belt and began teaching Karate at NYU. I was a skinny, shy thirteen-year old and Robert asked me to join him one night. At the start of my first class, Robert wanted to show his students a sweeping technique and asked me to throw a punch at him. The next thing I knew, I was flying through the air and landed squarely on my ass. It hurt physically, emotionally and was humiliating yet it made plain my brother's fighting skills and his competitive spirit.

Classes then moved to my cousin Rod's basement on Saturday mornings. Our group consisted of Rod, (who would grow up to become one of the world's top rock drummers) with nine of his friends and me. The first Kata we learned was Seiyunchin with slow, deliberate movements coordinated with strong breathing. We also did free fighting. It was brutal. During one class Robert had Randy and Paul free fight each other. Randy was a stocky 5'8 teen and Paul was about 6'2. Paul liked to kick a lot since he had long legs. One kick caught Randy in his right hand and broke it. Angry and visibly shaken, Randy stopped fighting and showed Robert his injured hand. Robert looked at it and said, "Suppress your emotions and don't get angry! One point to Paul, keep fighting". Holding his broken hand like a crane head, Randy kept fighting and won the bout.

Chapter 2: My Beginnings

I learned that Karate was for fighting and fighting only and that you never surrender to emotion or pain. I also learned that Robert had indeed come from a very tough Dojo. The classes lasted a couple of years until Robert moved on with his life.

The Green Hornet TV show, starring Bruce Lee as Kato, debuted in 1966 and introduced a strange Chinese fighting system to America. I watched every episode sitting at the edge of my seat waiting for the masked Kato to kick some bad guys ass with his powerful punches and crazy kicks. I was hooked on Kung Fu.

Then in 1970, my friends and I headed down to Chinatown to watch the Kung Fu movies, which had become wildly popular. Everybody wanted to be "Kung Fu fighting". My interest in the Martial Arts was at an all-time high.

During my freshman year of high school in 1972, I was mugged by three guys who stole my watch. It was a surreal moment as in my mind I calmly went through a series of punches and kicks I had learned from Robert. The problem was that it all happened in my head and not my body. As I imagined myself kicking their asses, I heard a voice in my head say "you know Karate and will be arrested for excessive force"... and I froze. It was over in a second. A policeman and I ended up chasing the boys down and retrieving the stolen goods. I may have had my stuff back, but my ego and confidence were severely bruised.

Following that incident, I joined Toyotaro Miyazaki's Shotokan Dojo in Flushing Queens. The style was Japanese and very linear. The classes were rigid and hard, run in a militaristic way. The Sensei, Toyotaro Miyazaki, was a highly skilled Karate man and fighter from Japan. He showed no emotion, just toughness and a no nonsense approach to teaching his students. I wasn't fond of this hard style and quit after just three months.

Two years later, Robert introduced me to Grand Master Seikichi Toguchi's Shorei-Kan Karate which was brought to New York City several years earlier by two of Toguchi's top students, Shoichi Yamamato and Akira Kawakami. (The only GoJu being taught in New

KARATE: BENEATH THE SURFACE

York City before that was by Maestro Peter Urban, one of the original GI's to study Karate in Japan.) Additionally, Master Toguchi sent a senior student from Japan to New York City to act as USA Representative of Shorei-Kan and run the NYC Dojo. The Shorei-Kan Representative was a tall lanky man who claimed to be from a Samurai family.

I accompanied Robert to watch a demonstration at the Shorei-Kan Dojo Headquarters in Rockefeller Center and what I saw both fascinated and excited me. I watched powerful and graceful Kata performed. I saw men standing toe to toe slugging it out with the hardest punches and kicks one could throw in an all out controlled brawl ending with one guy getting thrown by his head and rolling out of it to escape a broken neck. It was awe-inspiring. A few years down the road, this would be the style of Karate highlighted in my brother's movie "The Karate Kid".

I, of course, joined on the spot. GoJu-Ryu is a similar Karate style to the Isshin-Ryu that Robert had taught me, so I took to it easily.

The Shorei-Kan Dojo and the Representative, presented Karate as more than just fighting. There was an air of spirituality permeating the Dojo. This meshed with my increasing curiosity about consciousness raising and reaching a state of enlightenment. During this time while attending college, I learned Transcendental Meditation and practiced the sitting meditation, two times a day. I also trained at the Dojo three nights a week. One of the methods of Shorei-Kan was to approach the Kata as moving meditation, as well as developing fighting skills. The sitting meditation and moving meditation complemented each other, but in my heart I always felt there was more.

While I fell in love with the style and Dojo, I was confused. The Dojo had been in business for years, yet there were very few Black Belts training. I heard stories about students who followed a very skilled guy with a bad reputation who had quit the school a year earlier. Nonetheless, I had found a style I loved and trained there for the next eight years, earning a second degree Black Belt in Karate and a first degree Black Belt in Kobudo (Okinawan weapons).

Chapter 2: My Beginnings

Then in 1980, I discovered that the image the Representative showed the world was not his true self. This man allowed his students to put him on a spiritual pedestal, but he did not practice what he preached. Without going into embarrassing detail, he was, in reality, a man who betrayed me emotionally and spiritually. He violated the Martial Virtues (page 39) in the worst way possible and he did it on the Dojo floor, under the shrine!

I walked into his office and confronted him. In response to my confrontation, he meekly said, "I can't teach you anymore, it's too hard."

I was enraged, not only from the betrayal, but because he contradicted the very heart of his teachings. I sternly replied through my emotional pain, "For eight years, all I've heard on the Dojo floor is – if it's hard, try harder! The art," I continued, "is more important to me, and *you* are the only one who is teaching this art in New York City, so you *will* teach me." So I stayed and he taught, but the lesson I learned about trust and betrayal burned deeply.

A year later, the Representative closed the Dojo with very short notice and abandoned all his students. His betrayal resulted in no Dojo, no one in charge and a tarnished reputation for himself and Shorei-Kan. This was certainly not how I envisioned an enlightened man would behave. He showed no integrity whatsoever. It angered and shocked me and taught me a valuable lesson: Put no one on a pedestal.

Brokenhearted, I searched for a new Dojo to call home. I craved the spiritual foundations I thought I had in Shorei-Kan. Kendo caught my attention and I joined Reverend Kan's Ken Zen Institute in Manhattan. Not being one to tip toe into something new, I splurged and bought a full Kendo armor set, which set me back $500. Unfortunately, after a few months of intense training, often leaving me black and blue from neck to waist, I found that Kendo wasn't for me. So I sold the armor and with the money bought my wife a nice yellow sapphire ring!

Still craving a Dojo to call home, I rented a dance studio in Manhattan one night a week for the Shorei-Kan Black Belts to continue training hoping we could restart the Shorei-Kan Dojo. I also started a school in Fresh Meadows Queens, NY along with my Shorei-Kan friends. We had 150 students, ranging from seven to seventy years old.

After one of our Fresh Meadows classes, a student informed me that a man was teaching the same Karate as Shorei-Kan in a dance school in Manhattan, and that man knew all about the Representative. Was he that guy with the bad reputation who had quit Shorei-Kan just a year before I joined? Were the rumors true? I had to find out.

Kayo Killed My Karate

My curiosity led me to meet Kow Loon Ong, better known as Kayo, my current tutor and good friend, who opened my eyes to the true nature of GoJu-Ryu and the meaning of the phrase "mind, body and spirit".

As kismet would have it, Kayo was teaching in a dance studio around the corner from where the Shorei-Kan class was held on the same night. Shorei-Kan's class was between 6PM and 9PM. Kayo's class was from 9PM to Midnight. So one night after the Shorei-Kan class ended, two friends and I walked around the block to see for ourselves.

Entering his Dojo, I saw not one Karate Gi (uniform). His students were in shorts and tee shirts, not one Karate belt in sight. They were practicing the same Taisho Daruma, Kata, Bunkai and Kiso I had learned at Shorei-Kan. Kayo greeted me and my two friends with a huge smile.

CHAPTER 2: *MY BEGINNINGS*

He told us of his time at Shorei-Kan, confirming what I had suspected. Kayo was that guy with the bad reputation who had quit the year before I had joined. Seems he too was betrayed by the Representative, forcing him to leave the school he had helped build and had loved with all his heart.

Kayo was a short pure Chinese man (actually "Han Yan," as a descendent from the Han Dynasty), very well built and very strong. His wrists were as thick as his biceps and his hands were so well developed, they were more paw-like than human. We talked for a while, and then everyone performed a Kata in a welcoming ceremony. After seeing our Kata, Kayo told us that we were like nice shiny guns – our Kata were pretty and polished, but we had no bullets, meaning we had no firepower in our techniques. We didn't understand him, so he demonstrated.

Kayo stood with his feet shoulder width apart, hands loosely at his sides and said, "Hit me in my chest as hard as you can". I planted my stance and slammed him, and to my surprise he didn't move, my punch simply bounced off of him. He said in a mocking and condescending voice, "That's all you got?" and blew a kiss in my direction! My two friends tried as well with the same results. Kayo then gave us two thick Yellow-Pages books to hold against our own chests and told us to plant ourselves best we could. Kayo just stood there in no particular stance, relaxed, placed his fist on the front of the books and breathed out. Each of us went flying back several feet and it felt like an electric shock went through us. We had never felt anything like that before. Kayo said, "See... shiny guns, no bullets".

That was the moment Kayo killed my Karate,
...and opened my eyes.

At Shorei-Kan, we were told, "don't ask, just do" (the concept of Shu Ha Ri and Mochi Bun - detailed in Chapter 4). Here with Kayo, I found myself with an advanced Martial Artist who was more than happy to share everything he knew. We asked if he would teach us, and in the spirit of *the old ways*, he replied, "you already have a teacher (meaning my brother Robert). I will be your tutor."

I spent the next six months asking question after question, usually not even getting out of the dressing room, much to the chagrin of his students who, for all intents and purposes, lost their teacher for months on end. I owe them all my gratitude for bearing with me and remaining my friends. Each now is a skilled Martial Artist in his own right.

Kow Loon Ong

Kow Loon Ong (Kayo) emigrated with his parents from China to the rough and tumble South Bronx, New York City in the 1950's. Kayo was regularly bullied and his family harassed. His participation in the Martial Arts was not driven by a desire to reach enlightenment or grand stature. His desire was to stay alive. His body has the scars of multiple knife wounds to prove it.

Kayo was a scrawny kid who set out to learn how to beat anyone who dare attack him. He trained his mind, body and spirit to a high level and in addition to being a master of GoJu-Ryu, he has extensive experience and wide ranging knowledge of several Kung Fu styles. Consistent with his assertion that a Martial Artist must seek balance in his life just as he seeks balance in his body, Kayo is a successful businessman, entrepreneur and a Federal Aviation Administration certified mechanic.

He is surrounded by a wonderful family and considers all his students part of his extended family. His doors are always open.

CHAPTER 2: *My Beginnings*

Kayo's understanding of the art of GoJu-Ryu is outstanding and he can use it at will in any encounter. I saw this first hand as advanced students from various fighting systems came to the Dojo to challenge him. Kayo always required them to attack him with anything they desired, with full power and with the intent to damage. In every instance, Kayo responded to the attack with a technique straight out of one of the GoJu Kata. Every single time. He subdued everyone, often with the visitor on the ground in excruciating pain or unconscious. Most of these men ended up joining the Chi-I-Do organization and becoming Kayo's students and friends.

While Kayo has aged, he has changed almost nothing of what his teachers taught him. He still teaches "the old way". His Martial Arts and his ability to transmit the art have reached a high level. I have watched him gracefully transform from a fighter to teacher, incorporating spiritualism and extreme character building into his lessons.

Kayo is an inspiration and continues to improve the lives of his students each and every day.

Leaving Shorei-Kan

In 1982, the Shorei-Kan school run by Sensei Tomoaki Koyabu in Vancouver, Canada, held a celebration commemorating their tenth year anniversary. Master Toguchi was invited from Japan to teach. My friends and I decided to attend. I had seen Master Toguchi perform Kata at the demonstration in New York in 1974 but had never trained under him.

Moreover, at this point, I had been studying with Kayo for a year and found many of his techniques differed from the Shorei-Kan Representative's. This was a chance for me to see how the Master did things and who was correct.

As we performed Kata the Representative had taught us, Toguchi corrected our techniques, instructing us to do them precisely as Kayo had taught. When we did them Kayo's way, Toguchi just passed us by. It was shocking. Then we did Sanseiru Kata. At a critical point in the Kata, my friends and I stepped back while all of Koyabu's students stepped forward. Toguchi stopped the class and approached us. "Who taught that to you?" he angrily asked. We answered, "the Representative!" The Master shook his head, walked away muttering the Representative's name in disgust. We asked which way was correct? Toguchi pointed at the other students, and in his raspy Okinawan voice replied, "that way!".

We had our answer. Much of what I had studied for eight years at Shorei-kan under the Representative was wrong. Kayo's way was correct. During the last dinner with the Master, we asked if he knew Kayo. He looked up in the air saying Kayo's name over and over, then said "Ah yes, a short Chinese fellow! Ahhhh, very good Karate!" We asked if it was ok to study with Kayo and he said, "No problem." We happily traveled back to New York the next day.

A day after we returned, we received notice from Master Toguchi that we had to choose between studying with Kayo or leaving Shorei-Kan. I was one of the top seniors at Shorei-Kan. Kayo was fifteen years my senior and his Karate was the clearly the same as Master Toguchi's, who was in direct lineage to Masters Higashionna, Miyagi and Higa. My choice was clear. I chose to leave Shorei-Kan and study exclusively from Kayo.

Beshert

In Yiddish, the word "beshert" means "destiny". It is often used to describe one's divinely foreordained spouse or soulmate.

I met my wife Marina on a blind date.

The moment I saw her I felt as if I had known her my entire life. On our first date we recounted our lives and, never having crossed paths, I said "I know you from my future!" She, of course, thought I was crazy. But here we are decades later still happily married with three amazing and accomplished adult children.

Marina and I had been dating for just two weeks. I was head over heels in love and knew I had met my beshert. She was beautiful, in great physical shape and smart as a whip. She had blond hair, crystal blue eyes and a dazzling personality, like a firecracker on the Chinese New Year.

CHAPTER 2: *MY BEGINNINGS*

One night we had a disagreement and it exploded into an all-out verbal brawl. I stormed out of my house to circle the block and cool off. During this walk, I had a moment of self-awareness. I had never become so angry in all my life! Not by a long shot.

Suddenly I realized that this woman, this amazingly wonderful person, had the ability to reach deep down into my soul and touch me where no one had touched me before. She had shaken me to my core and I knew she was the person I wanted to spend the rest of my life with.

That night I asked her be my bride. We married in 1983.

Marina and I started our own production company, Kamen Entertainment Group, Inc., in New York City in 1987, with 11,000 square feet of recording studios in Times Square. We have produced thousands of radio, television, fitness, and live entertainment programs.

Since the age of four, Marina was trained by New York's best dance, music, and acting teachers. To supplement her income as a young performer, in 1980, she taught as a Master Trainer at Body Design by Gilda, New York City's first aerobic studio.

Marina is now an accomplished violinist, composer, director, singer and choreographer. She has written, produced and performed hundreds of songs and more than fifty albums. Her voice can be heard on countless television and radio commercials and she is known as MARINA, performing in the dance clubs of New York City's nightlife scene.

As a result of her training, Marina has perfected the expression and communication of intense emotions through physical movement and vocalization. She showed me how to tap into this well of power that has resulted in a deeper understanding of my own art form.

Although I had been taught to suppress my emotions in Karate class, the idea of *expressing emotions through Kata* was planted and began to take root in my mind. After all, one of the most important decisions in my life was based on an emotion – to make Marina my wife!

Emotion and Kata… hummm. It was something to think about.

Fix It In The Mix

I was a recording engineer for ten years prior to meeting Marina, and my approach had always been to "fix it in the mix", which means it's the engineer's job to correct any problems encountered while recording during the post-production process.

Typically, in a recording session for a commercial, we record between 20-70 "takes" of the script being read. One day, during a recording for a new car commercial, Marina gave the actor a direction that had nothing to do with the script. She described a scene, which gave the actor a particular internal experience and feeling. The very next take was perfect, with no editing needed. I was astonished and learned a valuable lesson.

I came to realize that what made a production superior was not my engineering work, but the actor's performance. Without that, the end result, no matter how hard I worked to "fix it in the mix", was often missing that *special something* that moved audiences, which is essential in making a "hit". This knowledge created a major shift in how I worked.

An actor's performance stirs the audience's emotions, not some turning of a console knob or flipping of a machine switch. The emotional content of that performance is the key to a superb production. Great actors are in touch with their emotions and are trained to convey those intense feelings. And so with Marina's guidance, my focus in the studio shifted from technical to emotional. My job had turned more towards creating a nurturing environment for actors to allow them the freedom to explore their art form, while I then sat back and captured it on tape. I discovered that the need to "fix it in the mix" decreased dramatically.

It was a turning point in my professional life that helped Kamen Entertainment Group win numerous industry awards and set the stage for my future discoveries in the Martial Arts.

Chapter 3: *Cultivating The Way*

*"There is no gate on the way of life that refuses entrance
to those who want to pass through.
If you want to go somewhere, take any way,
there are thousands and all are equal.
If luckily you succeed in your goal,
the way will disappear and you will become the way."*

*This is an old Zen Buddhist saying. I think of it often as I practice my Karate. Great forests develop from a single seed.
Tall buildings start with one brick.*

The same holds true for Karate.

Along my path I have had many realizations about the training and all that goes into it. These are several of those revelations which shaped my thoughts and feelings. Without these fundamental concepts, I would never have found my way.

Chapter 3: Cultivating The Way

Paths to Enlightenment

I have chosen Karate as my path to enlightenment and way of life. These are a few of the key concepts to which I adhere:

1. Do not strike anyone and do not let others strike you;

2. Realize that Karate techniques are deadly and must be performed that way;

3. Expand and contract the body, mind and spirit;

4. Breathe in through the nose and out through the mouth;

5. Breathe downward into your Dantian, a spot about three inches below the navel;

6. Sink energy down through your feet while pulling power up. Project power out through your hands while drawing energy in;

7. Kata have themes, including emotional ones;

8. Emotions are the most powerful energies we have and should be infused into technique;

9. Always be conscious of Mandala, Mantra and Mudra as key components of Kata (see Chapter 4);

10. Touch the divine through Kata;

11. The Kata opening and closing is a ritual prayer;

12. Always nourish and harmonize the mind, body and spirit;

13. If you find something is hard to do, try harder. Never give up;

14. Proper instruction and repetition are keys to understanding.

My Dojo

The Dojo is a place to learn "The Way". It is where one goes to learn, study and practice Karate. I have visited many Dojo's of other styles and teachers. All too many are full of bloated egos and distractions. The most popular of the large "McDojos" are adorned with fancy decorations reminiscent of Japan's great feudal days and littered with training tools and implements. There is often a strong sense of superiority amongst the students.

My Dojo however, is different; it is a humble place.

Like the Jewish temple my father took me Saturday mornings for prayer, I enter the Dojo with a sense of wonder. It is in a New York City public school cafeteria in front of Kayo's home, only steps from his door. There is no sign outside and no indication it is a Dojo. Inside there are no pictures of masters, no plaques or awards on the walls. There are no shelves or cases full of shiny trophies. There is no Hojo Undo equipment, no weights, no heavy bag, no speed bag, no makiwara (punching post) and no wall of weapons. No shrines and no nametags hanging. No statues of Buddha, Dragons or Foo Dogs. The floor is not wood, but hard linoleum with the feel of dirt on bare ground. There are no shoji screens and no rice paper walls. No Kanji anywhere to be seen. Neither showers nor formal dressing rooms. Not one mirror in the place and the doors are always open during class. There is no signup fee, no monthly fee and no promotion fee, just $35 for an annual membership. Students pay $10 a class that helps pay for the rental of space, if they can afford it. Karate Gis and belts are optional. Sometimes we do a full formal class, other times, group and individual training. We never know what to expect. The atmosphere is relaxed, not militaristic.

The relaxed atmosphere of my Dojo and selfless support by Kayo has stretched the boundaries of my experience and has allowed my spirit to soar.

Sacred Space

As in a temple, I consider the Dojo floor to be a *sacred space*. It is where all the answers to Karate can be found. It is like the canvas on which an artist paints. Upon entering and leaving, we bow to show our respect for all the Dojo signifies and all of the knowledge we gain there.

In a traditional Karate school, before class begins students use wet rags to run up and down the floor cleaning away any dirt left over from the previous training session. It is a cleansing of sorts, simultaneously exercising the students' bodies and teaching them that the floor is a special place requiring special attention.

In our Dojo, the school janitor cleans the floor prior to every class as part of the rental fee. This does not excuse the students from policing the floor to make sure every last piece of paper or dust is removed.

A clean floor is a pure floor; a clean slate upon which we write our Kata. It is a sacred space upon which we train our body, mind and spirit in harmony with each other and the world around us.

Mirrors

We don't have any mirrors in our Dojo. In the past, when we rented dance studios for training, we faced away from the mirrors. There is a very sound, biological reason for not training with mirrors. It is called *Proprioception*, or the sense of the relative position of neighboring parts of the body and strength of effort being employed in movement. Proprioception allows us to know where our body parts are in space just by "feeling". Proprioceptors are sensory receptors found within our joints that receive stimuli from within the body that respond to position and movement. They become more sensitive as we train Kata. This is vital in any physical art form, such as dance or Karate.

When we don't have a mirror for visual feedback, we need to depend on how we *feel*. Caught in the street in a self-defense situation, do you have visual feedback? No. You just have to know where you are and where you are going. This is the best way to train. Master your own body in space and you can master many other things in life.

Ambiguity

I have found that most events can be interpreted many different ways. For instance, take my first day of Karate class with Robert. I always looked up to my big brother as someone who would protect me from all harm; yet there I sat on my butt, humiliated and hurt by him throwing me across the room just to make a point to his students, and perhaps to me.

Was his goal to humiliate me, hurt me, show me who was the boss or to intimidate his students? Perhaps it was just to teach what a throw was or to perfect his own technique. Maybe he was actually showing me love by teaching me a valuable lesson - to learn to protect myself. Perhaps all of the above.

We are trained to interpret people's actions and events through pre-defined filters or beliefs we developed based on our personal experiences and influences. Consequently, many times what we think is truth or reality is just personal perception based on preconceived notions. These preconceptions frequently lead us to false conclusions leaving us confused by a person's behavior or disappointed by unexpected outcomes. What we thought was reality was merely an illusion – an interpretation of our mind… or just *delusion*.

This does not happen on the Dojo floor. Things *are* what they appear to be. You can either do or not. There is no ambiguity when your block doesn't work and you get hit. No ambiguity. Your technique either works or it doesn't. You are either doing Kata correctly or not. You are behaving within the Dojo rules or not. You are either a junior or a senior. There are no greys. It's all either black or white. No ambiguity.

It is actually a simple way to view life. You can either do something or not. There is no such thing as *trying*. Trying to do something is not the same as getting it done. You can try forever and never get it done.

There was really no ambiguity on the Dojo floor that day at NYU. The bottom line is that Robert swept my leg; I flew and ended up on my ass. Everything I thought about it, all the reasons I conjured as to why he did it, was just delusion.

Chapter 3: *Cultivating The Way*

This is one of the things I cherish about going to class and Karate practice. You either can do it or not. There is no doubt, confusion or delusion.

Alone In A Crowd

I sit on the Dojo floor before class, stretching and trying to clear my mind of the day's events. I listen to the other students yack away, talking about this or that and wonder how they could be missing out on the opportunity to quiet themselves and focus inwardly before class begins.

On the Dojo floor during practice, I am surrounded by other teachers and students. Everyone is engaged in warm ups, Kata, Kiso or Bunkai. Sometimes the entire class practices Kata together or in small groups. This is similar to my experience going to Temple with my father, with rows of old bearded men standing in their black garb all bowing and raising their hands in prayer together, yet each praying for themselves, alone with their God.

No matter how many people are on the Dojo floor when I stretch quietly before class, I am alone. When I practice my Kata, I am alone. While I am aware of everyone on the Dojo floor, my focus is inward.

This is my meditation. The Dojo is my temple.

Martial Virtues

When you study Martial Arts, you can attain great power over others. In order to reach the higher spiritual levels, a code of conduct must be followed. The following is the code of conduct, or "Virtues" of Kayo's Chi-I-Do Organization that everyone in my Dojo follow:

1. **Courtesy:** Respect all people and respect yourself;

2. **Loyalty:** Be loyal to the organization, the Sensei or instructors, classmates, family and friends;

3. **Kindness:** Refrain from making negative statements about anyone and always strive for what is good and correct, working toward harmony among people and always keep in mind others' well being;

4. **Courage:** Never surrender to the enemy. Correct what you know is wrong and succeed in one's goals or intentions. Utilize your skill to help and defend the defenseless, our family, friends and our honor;

5. **Justice:** One needs to know that we are all equal, to understand that we all have weakness. Never be arrogant and always be humble. Refrain from giving unnecessary displays of one's abilities;

6. **Discipline:** Refrain from violence. Always exercise self-control and always finish what is started;

7. **Strength:** Be strong always! Develop an indomitable spirit and will to be like steel, for this is the way of the Martial Arts;

8. **Honor:** Refrain from doing wrong which can shame our Dojo and oneself, for we represent the heritage of correctness, which those before us have preserved. To be honorable, one must be honorable to others;

9. **Truth:** Be true to yourself and others, for deceit and lies breed negativity and darkness in one's mind, body and spirit.

****

These Virtues are not just for the Dojo floor. I carry them with me throughout my life. I follow them in dealings with my family, friends, co-workers, clients and even strangers.

They are like signposts along the path, pointing in the correct way to behave. Too often these Virtues are not taught in Karate Dojos and students' lives suffer an imbalance. Karate is not just about fighting. It is also about living a healthy and balanced life.

These Virtues are the spiritual bedrock of the Martial Arts.

CHAPTER 3: CULTIVATING THE WAY

Integrity

This is a big one... Integrity. What does that mean and why is it so important?

According to the dictionary, Integrity can mean several things:

1. Adherence to moral and ethical principles, soundness of moral character and honesty;

2. The state of being whole, entire, or undiminished to preserve the integrity of the empire;

3. A sound, unimpaired, or perfect condition such as the integrity of a building's structure.

All three definitions relate to our Martial Arts. However, for my purpose I'll focus on the first meaning as it relates to *compassion*. Being compassionate to someone who has wronged you and forgiving him or her creates a moral bond that should not be broken. To be forgiven for wrongdoing creates a responsibility on the part of the forgiven to not repeat the behavior that caused the harm in the first place. All too often, when someone forgives us for poor behavior, instead of taking it to heart and changing our ways, we merely go about our business as before.

We ignore the special gift the forgiver has extended and once again cause the same problems. It is like doing a technique poorly, being corrected, and then doing it the wrong way again, over and over. Do you really think you will be corrected forever? At some point your teacher will give up on you and stop trying to improve your techniques. Then why bother coming to class and practicing anymore?

Changing your behavior and acting with integrity, thereby acting with a higher code of ethics, honor or morals, becomes your responsibility. To act otherwise is to insult the one who offered compassion and forgiveness.

Master Toguchi wrote about this in his essay titled "Thinking About Favor" from his book of essays "Zen And The Way Of The Warrior":

Karate: Beneath The Surface

> *"When we consider the meaning of the word "favor", we immediately tend to think of a relationship between a "giver" of a favor and the "receiver" of the favor. We know, for example, that in our society the giving of a favor often creates an obligation in the receiver to return the favor.*
>
> *Acceptance is a major ingredient in the Buddhist conception of favor. Doing favors is part of the duty of anyone who has achieved the State of Compassion. A favor is done without any intention of creating an obligation to return it. A favor should be done merely because another being requires it. It should be forgotten by the one who gives it. If the giver puts any pressure on the receiver, he might actually create repulsion on the part of the receiver. This would entirely destroy the meaning of the word as far as Buddhists are concerned.*
>
> *On the other hand, although the giver of a favor must instantly forget it, the receiver must never do so. To forget a favor would be ingratitude and we talk of ungrateful persons as being beneath even dogs, which, as we know, return their owner's love with devotion and faithfulness. Ingratitude has always been considered a disgrace in the orient.*
>
> *Forgetting favors, and refusing to give favors with compassion, means losing touch with our human nature, with what it means to be human. It is this forgetting, this lack of recognition of the tie of common Humanity that binds us all, which creates Hell on earth, a Hell which traps and destroys saint and sinner alike.*
>
> *In the Martial Arts we trust each other and value and respect the human relationship the giving and receiving of favors creates. Before all else we revere human nature. Hard training and proficient techniques are not enough to become a Martial Artist respected by oneself and by others. We must also thoroughly understand and practice the meaning of favor."*

In my life, I have tried to act consistently, morally and ethically towards my family, friends, co-workers, clients, teachers and strangers. I extend that to treating myself with integrity as well. I also try to bring this concept into my Kata. I strive to keep integrity in my physical form and be fully engaged while running through the Kata with mind, body and spirit. I see so many students unconsciously doing Kata, or perhaps just focusing on a single technique or stance, ignoring everything else.

CHAPTER 3: *CULTIVATING THE WAY*

To do Kata and live with integrity is difficult and requires the highest level of awareness.

Trust

"Wanna buy a bridge? What? ... You don't trust me?" Trust is a tricky thing. Trust must be earned. It takes years to build and a mere second to destroy. Trust is fragile and needs to be protected and nurtured. Trust is all-important in relationships between family members, friends and co-workers. Trust is essential between business partners and nations. It is the centerpiece for getting along and getting things done. Losing trust is terrible. When someone you trust sticks a knife in your back, it is the ultimate betrayal. Trust in the Martial Arts is primary. This is the lesson I learned firsthand during my Shorei-Kan days with the Representative. He betrayed my trust and it has haunted me to this day.

Open your eyes and learn whom you can trust.

A key tenet of the Martial Arts is that your teacher is never wrong. The Japanese word for teacher is "Sensei" meaning "one who has gone before". We students follow the path our teachers have followed to be what they are today. Once you start questioning their teachings and stop trusting them, you will never advance in their art. Now, this is not to say that you should blindly trust a teacher, for there are plenty of charlatans out there who just want to take your money. They come in all sizes and shapes with all sorts of belts and titles. Seek out a teacher who earns and deserves your trust. As I found out, blind trust can get you hurt.

You must also trust in your technique. The person who questions whether their techniques will work in a fight has already lost. Many sequences in Kata have us moving into the attack to defend ourselves. This takes tremendous trust in your training and courage to pull off difficult techniques under the pressure against bladed weapons like knives. Practice your techniques until you trust they will work.

Without trust your Martial Art is useless.
However, blind trust can get you killed.

Mindset

When I enter the Dojo, I leave the troubles of the world outside. I forget about problems I've encountered, any business I've done, and activities I've engaged in. I also leave behind any anticipation of what I will be doing in the next few hours on the Dojo floor. And one of the most important things I do before practice is dropping my Ego. Entering the Dojo is like dying, only to be reborn again upon leaving after class.

In the Dojo during class, I try to be like an empty cup with no bottom, letting the knowledge pour in. I never let my cup fill or overflow.

When I train, I keep my mind open to all possibilities. My thoughts flow freely. I train myself to increase my ability to understand the techniques within the Kata and thereby increase my ability to understand other things outside of Kata.

In the beginning stages of learning Kata, students are rarely told what the movements actually mean. It is up to the student, through endless repetition, to understand what the techniques are and how they are applied.

A student must always train with a beginner's mind, always hungry for knowledge and excited at every new discovery. It doesn't matter how long you have been studying the arts, you must always keep a beginner's mindset if you are to advance, flourish and evolve in the Martial Arts.

Chi

What is Chi?

The ancient Chinese described Chi as "life force". They believed Chi permeated everything, linking them to their surroundings and the Universe. They likened Chi to the flow of energy around and through the body, forming a cohesive and functioning unit. By understanding its rhythm and flow they created exercises and treatments that provided stability and longevity.

The human body absorbs Chi like a sponge and projects Chi around us, like a light bulb glowing. When your Chi interacts with someone else's, as when they get physically very close to you, you experience a good or bad feeling depending on how your Chi mixes. For instance, as two lovers come close, the feelings are good. When two enemies get close, the feelings are tumultuous.

Traditional Chinese Medicine states that when your Chi is blocked, you get sick. When your Chi is flowing unimpeded, you are healthy and vital. We develop the ability to generate Chi throughout the body and project it outward through our Martial Arts.

Visualize a punch as an empty pipe. While the pipe is strong and can do great damage to anyone unlucky enough to be struck by it, imagine the force of the blow and the attendant damage if it is filled with cement or water. Being struck by a filled pipe will do much more damage than an empty pipe alone. Chi is like the cement or water. It fills the punching arm with power. Getting hit by a punch filled with flowing Chi is like being struck by lightning. It actually feels like an electric shock tracking through your body – as I experienced upon meeting Kayo.

The way to develop this Chi force is through performing Kata and, more specifically, Sanchin Kata and Tensho Kata.

You know your Chi is flowing when your hands and feet turn red.

Breathing

One day in the recording studio, I was producing a commercial for a big action movie. After having spent eight hours designing the sound, the writer began screaming about some insane changes he suddenly decided were absolutely necessary just minutes before our deadline. How did I deal with the pressure? I calmed myself by breathing, as I had learned in Karate class, and got the job done.

There is a right way and a wrong way to breathe. Typically, new students breathe high in their chest. You can see their shoulders rise as they breathe in and fall when they breathe out. When they exert themselves, the effects become exaggerated. This type of breathing causes several problems for the Martial Artist. First, it is shallow breathing. The student cannot fill his lungs to capacity and he cannot pressurize his body, which is required for Sanchin Kata (a Bible Kata of GoJu-Ryu), and power generation. Second, breathing in this manner telegraphs his breathing pattern. A skilled fighter will be able to see when his opponent breathes, giving him the advantage of timing his attack to coincide with the change of breath and resulting decrease in mobility.

Proper breathing occurs as the diaphragm drops and the lungs fill downward into the lower torso. Breathing this way allows the lungs to fill fully and the body to pressurize, generating Chi. Also, as you breathe downward, your belly and lower back expand like an inflated tire, not your chest and shoulders. This makes it difficult, if not impossible, for your opponent to see your breathing cycles and therefore makes the timing of his attacks much more difficult.

The Karate Belt comes in handy when learning how to breathe. When tying the belt, you should be able to slip two fingers between the belt and your waist. Upon breathing in and expanding your lower torso, the belt should tighten and squeeze your fingers. The belt acts like a feedback system, letting you know when you are breathing correctly. So always wear your belt tied properly when practicing.

Deep low breathing is essential to develop and generate Chi. Breathe downward and let your lower torso fill with air and expand. This method of breathing is also the preferred method of breathing for virtually all meditation. It helps calm the mind, body and spirit.

I always breathe this way, on and off the Dojo floor.

Breath As Spiritual Matter

In Karate training we are taught how to breathe – when you block, you breathe in, when you punch, you breathe out. The breath is always syncronized with a physical movement. However, there is a spiritual component that we overlook.

Carl Sagan, an American astronomer, cosmologist, astrophysicist, and author, said the following about breathing:

CHAPTER 3: *CULTIVATING THE WAY*

> *"Spirit comes from the Latin word: to breathe.*
> *What we breathe is air, which is certainly matter, however thin. Despite usage to the contrary, there is no necessary implication in the word "spiritual" that we are talking of anything other than matter. Science is not only compatible with spirituality; it is a profound source of spirituality. When we recognize our place in an immensity of light-years and in the passage of ages, when we grasp the intricacy, beauty and subtlety of life, then that soaring feeling, that sense of elation and humility combined is surely spiritual. So are our emotions in the presence of great art or music or literature, or of acts of exemplary selfless courage."*
>
> ~ Carl Sagan

If the air we breathe is thought of as just "matter", we are basically swimming in it, taking it in, transforming it within our bodies and expelling it. The air we breathe out is different than the air we breathe in. Many cells in our body participate in the transformation. The air we breathe out contains parts of us as a result of the transformation within us, like fingerprints left behind containing traces of our DNA. Anyone who breathes in the air we breath out is breathing in a piece of us and becomes part of them in the transformation process. In essence, the simple act of breathing in someone else's expelled breath creates an intimate relationship with that person.

In our art, we breathe out when we punch and breathe in when we block. The simple acts of punching and blocking create a physical intimacy through the touching of bodies. However, the act of breathing in the expelled air of the attacker as he punches, creates an intimacy on the biological level through the inhaling and transformation of the air contained in his breath. Perhaps through punching and blocking we become more like each other, and bond together merging as one, by sharing the air.

The idea that "sharing air" has a transformational effect puts a responsibility on each of us to breathe out the best possible air we can; to be able to transform the air while adding the fewest impurities. This is where practicing our art comes in. By eating well, stretching and strengthening our bodies, sharpening our minds and raising our spirits, we change the quality of our breath and therefore, positively impact all around us who breathe in our expelled air.

The air we breathe in at the Dojo is a mixture of all the air people around us breathe out. We are all engaged in a process of purifying ourselves through Kata practice and hence purifying our expelled breath. This is one reason why group Kata feels so good and has such beneficial effects.

One last thought on sharing air: If you have any kind of infectious respiratory illness, such as a cold or flu, do not practice Martial Arts with others. You will be sharing those germs, too.

Kiai

You often hear screaming coming out of a Karate Dojo. Those screams and shouts are called "Kiai". Why do we make all that noise?

Common knowledge in Karate is that a Kiai is a shout made at certain points of Kata to help unify the body and spirit. The secondary use is to supposedly "scare" your opponent.

It is not so common knowledge that there are many more Kiai in Kata than you have been taught. Kururunfa Kata, for instance, has two very different Kiai in the "full nelson release" section – "Ha" and "Hey".

The concept of Mudra, Mantra and Mandala (detailed in Chapter 4) illustrate that Kiai (Mantra) is more than just a shout at a few points in the Kata. Each hand position (Mudra) has its own Kiai within the overall pattern (Mandala) of the Kata. For instance, the Kiai of Sanchin Kata is the loud, deep breathing and "locks" at the end of each movement. Also, in Shisochin Kata, the single elbow drop is accompanied with a "humph" as you drop. This concept of Kiai is foreign to most Karateka, but once you approach Kata as Mudra, Mantra and Mandala, you see that there are many Kiai. Certain Kung Fu schools have many specific Kiai for specific techniques as well as for their Chi-Gong exercises.

CHAPTER 3: *CULTIVATING THE WAY*

The sonic vibrations of Kiai cannot be overlooked. As a sound engineer, I learned about the emotional impact sound can have. Think of a scary movie, like Psycho or Jaws. The impact of these soundtracks was part of the success of these films. Or think about the excitement generated by the massive high-fidelity sound systems at Rock concerts. The frequencies and amplitude of the sound seem to drive right through your body, vibrating and exciting every one of your cells.

Sound affects us emotionally. The quality of a Kiai can actually affect your opponent. Loud, clear and with authority, a Kiai can add considerable power to a technique or end a confrontation.

Kiai is a sound of Power.

I am always amazed when I watch students perform Kata in silence. My Kata is stronger when I Kiai loudly with energetic passion, release my energies, and free my spirit.

A Kata without Kiai is only two thirds of a Kata.

The Yin and Yang of Technique

For every action, there is a reaction. Each technique has a mirror image, or an application for a particular technique. For every attack, there is a defense. For every defense, there is an attack.

A technique and its mirror image application are considered to be a Yin / Yang relationship. The Yin represents the soft side (Ju) and the Yang represents the hard (Go).

And each technique has it's own Yin / Yang component. If you step in, the stance is considered Yang. If stepping back, it is Yin. But even within the moving forward or back there is some degree of Yin within the Yang and Yang within the Yin. That's why the small opposite color dots are there.

A major misconception of Yin / Yang is that they are static concepts as shown in the image. In reality, the two sections of the image swirl, interact and mix where the two distinct and separate characteristics seem to merge into a single swirl of grey. There is always Yin in the Yang and Yang in the Yin. This holds true for every technique in all of the Kata in GoJu-Ryu.

The concept of Yin / Yang also applies to the emotional and spiritual aspects of Kata. Deep love would be Yin and extreme rage would be considered Yang. Saintly intent would be Yin while evil intent would be considered Yang.

Repetition, Persistence and Patience

Things take time.
A cake takes time to bake. A pot of coffee needs time to percolate.
A Kata needs time to mature.

The key to mastery of anything is repetition, persistence and patience. There are many ceremonies that revolve around repetition – Meditation, Tea ceremonies, Archery, Kendo, Calligraphy, or reciting the Buddhist Sutras. They all require repetition, persistence and patience to achieve their goals.

The same holds true for Kata. The persistent repetition of Kata allows us the time to focus on the fine details of our Kata. Ultimately burning the movements into our body's memory so the techniques flow as Kata is performed in the absence of thought.

Think of Kata first learned as an infant learning to crawl. As you practice over time the Kata matures through adolescence, young adulthood, middle age and finally old age. It is the maturation of your physical techniques, your understanding of the Kata's strategies and the

CHAPTER 3: CULTIVATING THE WAY

Kata's emotional and spiritual elements that make Kata what it is for any student at any given time. The Kata you learn today is not the Kata you will do in 10, 20 or 30 years. That's why it takes many years of repetition to really know a Kata.

Too often, students are pushed through the Kata by teachers hungry for promotion-test dollars. Or the teacher creates a curriculum of so many Kata, that the student never really learns any one Kata in full. In today's world of the "ten-second attention span" our natural instinct is to become bored by repetition. Patience is lacking, so in the interest of keeping "paying" students happy, teachers throw many Kata, training methods and tournaments at the students, keeping them occupied, happy and the monthly dues flowing.

Repetition of Taisho Daruma, the two Bible Kata, the ten training Kata, and the eight Koryu Kata is all you need to achieve mastery of Karate. When you hear your teachers say "do it again", understand that he is saying this for your betterment as a person and as a Martial Artist.

The teacher that says "do it again" often and persistently, is a true teacher of "The Way".

Mushin

Mushin is a state of mindful mindlessness.

It is commonly understood that in Martial Arts, techniques happen in the absence of thought and that all emotion should be suppressed. This mindset, however, is more of a *mindlessness* rather than *mindfulness*. I do believe there is great wisdom in keeping cool heads during a fight. I also believe in the importance of training a technique properly thousands of times in order for it to become ingrained in our body, automatic and without thought. It sounds like pure reflex. This is Mushin. Mushin creates clarity of observation so we can respond quickly to any attack.

By practicing a technique repeatedly, we can always be in a state of Mushin and fight off any attack whether it's physical, verbal, emotional or spiritual. Mushin can also be applied to everyday tasks and hobbies.

Imagination

> *The world of reality has its limits; the world of imagination is boundless.*
> — Jean-Jacques Rousseau

Your techniques must be effective in combat or they are not correct. But how do you know when your posture and hand position of a particular technique is correct?

A bit of reverse engineering is required to unwind the technique and discover its mirror image. This process is called Bunkai and requires you to use your *imagination*.

Kata is more than a solo dance routine consisting of fighting techniques.

Kata is a fight with imaginary opponents.

As every Yin has a Yang and every Yang has a Yin, so does every physical technique in a Kata; for every movement, there is an imaginary opposing one. A physical punch has an imaginary block and visa-versa.

Imagination is a key component of Kata. The ability to visualize and interact with an imaginary opponent is how we learn to apply Kata techniques. Since our imagination is not limited by the physical, we can visualize multiple technique counterparts. For instance, one technique may have 3 or more imaginary scenarios.

Each imaginary scenario can result in small changes in how we do Kata techniques. This creates virtually unlimited ways to practice, study, and analyze Kata. By making fine adjustments in our Kata, we can fight an unlimited number of battles with better-trained opponents.

The *ability to imagine* can be trained to a high degree. Imagination fuels the creative artist and is at the heart of the Martial Arts.

Chapter 4: *Change*

> *Everything changes.*
>
> *Most of us don't like change, myself included.*
>
> *After all, if something works, why change it? Change hurts; it's uncomfortable and there are many unknowns.*
>
> *If there is one thing you can be certain of in life, it is that everything changes. You can either accept it or fight it.*
>
> *Accept it and you grow.*
>
> *Fight it and it can destroy you.*

CHAPTER 4: *CHANGE*

Growing Old

As I approached my fifty-eighth birthday, I began to think about my future. I had been out of class for several years after knee surgery, practicing on my own. Being honest with myself, I had not been stretching nor strengthening my body as I should have. I had not been practicing my Kata with a full heart nor with much strength.

My body had begun its decline into old age.

I decided to go visit my ninety-two year old mother who lived in a senior community in Florida, with the intention to see what happens to men in old age. What I found disturbed me greatly. The old men were either sitting around the pool deteriorating, or they followed their wives around to endless meetings carrying their bags. Many of them were in poor physical shape and would shuffle along, stiff and weak.

I became determined to not let that happen to me. I would not throw away all the years I had devoted to practicing Karate just because I had become lazy and hard training had become a distant memory of painful endurance.

Upon returning home from this trip, I expressed my feelings to Marina. She simply said "I've been telling you to go back to class. It's time you go." So, I put my pride aside and went back to Kayo's class.

Kayo welcomed me back as if no time had passed. But things were different. Not that the class was changed, but I had changed. My perceptions had changed. I suddenly realized that I was on a new path in the Dojo and with my Karate.

With a new emphasis and concentration on stretching and strengthening my body, I feel I am in better shape now in my 60's than I have ever been. My goal is to keep improving and to be in the best shape of my life on the day I die.

Thinking Outside The Box

My transformation was not due to anything Kayo said, taught or did. He hadn't changed anything. Class was exactly as I had remembered it. What had changed was how I looked at it. My belief system had shifted.

In order to explore the deeper aspects of Kata, I had to gain a new perspective and see things the way they really are. I had to ignore my filters and think outside the box in order to expand my beliefs past current acceptance and understanding. For instance, a student of boxing will understand the Kata from a boxer's point of view and reject anything that does not fit within that paradigm, such as kicking.

Many people understand Kata to be a series, or collection, of fighting techniques. Some will see the underlying fighting strategies. Others will see the health benefits of practicing Kata. However, thinking inside those boxes will surely limit your exploration of the Kata and rob you of what lies beneath the surface.

To grow, I had to open myself to new possibilities.

San Lorenzo Dojo

This is an entry in my journal after a visit to the Chi-I-Do Dojo in San Lorenzo, Puerto Rico, June 28-July 1, 2012:

"As I drove back from the airport today, my thoughts were on my visit to the Chi-I-Do Dojo in San Lorenzo, Puerto Rico. I was overcome by emotion, and now as I compose this, the tears are still streaming down my face. It is rare in one's life to discover a new home and a new family, and that is exactly what I found in San Lorenzo. I expected this trip to be an ordinary visit to a branch Dojo but what I experienced was an oasis of humanity nestled in a small town in the middle of a magical island nation. The smiling faces of my new friends are what I remember and it brings a profound joy to my heart. From the youngest student to the senior most teacher, each and every member of the school and their families and friends welcomed us with open arms and a burning desire to absorb the lessons Kayo, Lai, Bai, Gustavo and I offered. All practiced with the beginner's heart as sweat poured off their bodies.

CHAPTER 4: *CHANGE*

It was hot. It was humid. The workouts were long. No one complained. They wanted more and more and more. It was amazing and I will never forget it.

Saying goodbye was difficult because I felt like I had been training there for decades. Truly a home away from home.

I learned a valuable lesson in San Lorenzo, one that has nothing to do with how to block or punch or kick. I learned that the most powerful force we have to inject into our technique is "emotion".

Emotions change the world.

Emotions create new life with love and emotions take away life through hate. There is a fine line between love and hate, and that is where the power lies.

I practiced with Nelson, one of the teachers of San Lorenzo. He is a brute of a man; so damn powerful. Nelson laughs easily. He has no ego. Nelson is the embodiment of Okinawan GoJu-Ryu and a teacher of the art. While no one in the Dojo was arrogant, they were all very passionate about life. Everyone there smiled and laughed easily.

I don't think anyone can really master Karate without being able to easily laugh and cry, and in San Lorenzo they sure know how to do both.

I posted well over 300 pictures from the San Lorenzo Dojo classes onto the Chi-I-Do Facebook group. I tried to capture the relationships and emotions of the people there besides the usual "Karate class" pictures.

The best picture from the visit to the San Lorenzo Dojo is of a little boy sitting next to Kayo as Kayo was watching Chi-I-Do senior instructor Bai Zhou Zhu teach duck walking (which was pretty funny, as you can well imagine).

This boy was looking at Kayo with such awe, enjoyment and innocence. In one quick glance I think he expressed what we all feel about Kayo.

To me this special moment was reminiscent of Daniel-san looking up to his teacher Mr. Miyagi.

The Dojo gave Kayo a plaque honoring him. This is what it says:

> *"Sometimes it is difficult to express gratitude to someone who has given a lot without expecting anything in return; but the satisfaction of harvesting the fruits of what has been taught.*
>
> *Thank you for sharing your friendship, knowledge, wisdom and humor throughout all of these years."*
>
> *Given Today, July 1st, 2012*
>
> *Gilberto Melendez Felix Sensei and Nelson Borrero Sensei*

Friendship, knowledge, wisdom and humor are the hallmarks of a great martial artist and teacher, not just the ability to kill. Kayo does indeed give us those gifts everyday, and I am very honored to call Kayo my tutor and my friend. Thank you Kayo for inviting me on this journey and thank you to all my new friends, family and Chi-I-Do brothers and sisters of the San Lorenzo Dojo."

CHAPTER 4: *CHANGE*

The Great Oak Tree Sensei

I lived away from the Dojo for a few years in the mid 2000's. Everyday I would go outside my house and practice under a great old oak tree. Kayo had said that Shaolin means "forest" and that you can relate the trees in the forest to students in the Dojo.

Many of Kayo's lessons about breathing, expanding and contracting swirled through my mind during these workouts. I tried to become one with the tree to understand how the energy flowed.

As I was practicing Sanchin one morning, an acorn fell on my head and I had an epiphany.

A forest is made up of trees, some young, and some old. The old trees create safety for young saplings to take root, expand their trunks and branches as they reach for the sky. Their roots grow downward, giving stability to the soil. The same can be said for students in the Dojo. We are like individual trees, some older and more trained, who help the young students learn and grow in the art.

The roots of the tree grow downwards, into the earth to give the tree stability and allowing the branches to sway easily in the wind without the tree toppling over. The same is true in Kata. We press downward, gripping the floor with our toes, sending energy down, getting *heavy* in our stance and leaving our upper body relaxed so we can respond easily to changing attacks. However, another primary purpose of the tree's roots is to draw water and nutrients up from the soil. The roots dig deep and draw nourishment into the tree's trunk. We do the same when doing Kata. We root our stance and draw energy up into our core, or Dantian.

The branches of the tree grow up and outward toward the sun. The leaves capture and draw in sunlight and carbon dioxide needed for the tree's survival. So again, we have an outward expansion with a simultaneous inward absorption into the trunk of the tree. This same action occurs during Kata. Our arms, hands and fingers reach out, projecting energy, while simultaneously drawing in energy from our environment or our opponent into our Dantian.

Each tree in the forest is unique. Some are short, some tall. Some have strong rigid trunks that support strong solid branches and others flexible trunks able to withstand strong winds. Each tree grows shaped by the environment in which it grows.

As each tree is unique, so are students in the Dojo. Each has his or her own qualities that they express through the art. Each Kata learned represents another branch on the tree and the deeper the understanding of the Kata, the more lush the branch. A well-developed Karate student is like a well-developed tree.

As for my preference? I prefer to be like the Great Oak, with its extensive root system, strong trunk, many large well developed branches that extend up and out evenly with lush foliage, able to produce a plethora of healthy and vital acorns.

Shu Ha Ri and Mochi Bun

Until I met Kayo, all of my instructors taught Kata without any explanation. They said, "Just do it this way, don't ask why." This was very frustrating for me, however, I did as I was told. Many students have experienced the same thing. After spending 40 years in the Martial Arts, they still didn't have a full book of knowledge. Perhaps their teacher

Chapter 4: *Change*

didn't like or trust them. Perhaps the teacher didn't know the full art and just wanted to keep the students coming back for the monthly dues and promotion test fees. Or perhaps the teacher followed the Japanese concepts of *Shu Ha Ri* and *Mochi Bun*.

"Shu", the first stage of Shu Ha Ri, concerns learning a Kata by following the movements without question. This stage can last a lifetime, leaving a student not knowing what he is doing and, therefore, never learning the full book of the art.

The second stage, "Ha", concerns experimenting with what has been learned. Many students after several years in the art reach this stage and many teachers encourage it. Most students, including teachers, never progress past the stage of "Ha".

The final stage, "Ri", the practitioner transcends the techniques and only concept remains. He is free to create his own techniques and Kata.

In fighting, the student will be able to flow from one technique to another, regardless of what Kata the technique comes from. This is an advanced stage very few achieve.

This concept can also be applied to use of Karate in a fight. The Shu stage would enable you to deal with any assault using your art. Applying the Ha stage you would *see* trouble coming and seek a way to avoid it by perhaps crossing to the other side of the street or turning and walking away. In the Ri stage you would not be consciously aware that there was any trouble, as you would subconsciously avoid being anywhere in the vicinity of trouble. It is the ultimate in fighting without fighting.

Shu Ha Ri is the bedrock of the concept of Mochi Bun, meaning "the ability to understand". When the answers to questions are not given in the Shu stage, the student must figure out what every movement in Kata means by using his imagination. As you progress through the Ha stage, you begin to develop the skill to understand how the techniques work. This ability to understand is then applied unconsciously in the Ri stage. Once you develop the ability to understand, you can apply it to all techniques and understand everything in *and* out of the Dojo.

The Go and the Ju in GoJu

I am going to suggest a different meaning of *Go* and *Ju* in GoJu-Ryu for purposes of this book.

Go is everything you can see and physically touch. In Kata this refers to all techniques and physical movements including breathing.

Ju is everything you can't see. In other words, your attention, focus, Chi flow, mindset, fighting strategies, emotions and spirit.

I look at a Kata as if it were a building.

Stances are the foundation and steel beams; techniques are the walls, windows, ceilings, pipes, wires and floors. A strong Kata is like a strong building. It is the *Go* of GoJu. Everything you can touch and see.

But the building does not exist just to be a building.

The *purpose* of the building is for people to live or work, shop or be entertained. Each person has a life intertwined with others, through deep connections. They are like the *Ju* of GoJu. While the physical of the Kata is the building (Go), the emotional and spiritual side of Kata is like the lives that occupy and use the building (Ju). Ju is also the water that flows through pipes, not the pipes themselves. Ju is the electricity that flows through the wires, not the wires themselves. Ju is the people *using* the building, not the building itself.

Chapter 4: *Change*

The building has no purpose if there are no people using it. It is the same for Kata. A Kata without emotion and spirit is just an athletic activity, or "skin and bones" Karate. If you do not infuse emotion and spirit into your Kata, you are doing one half of a Kata. It's like listening to a song with lyrics, but no melody.

Music and Kata

Kayo had spoken often about doing Kata to music. It helps develop the rhythm and feelings of a Kata. When I told this to Marina she said: "Duh! That's what I have been telling you for years. Why don't you do Kata to music, it's like a dance, isn't it? Music can help you *feel* it."

Music has been an integral part of the human experience going back millennia. Music can stir the emotions, soothe the soul or ignite a riot. Since the dawn of Man, humans have moved their bodies to the rhythm of music from beating tree logs to symphony orchestras.

Indian, Chinese and Okinawan dance share many similarities to Martial Arts. Hidden in the traditional movements of these dance cultures are fighting techniques. The same applies to the Hula dances in Hawaii. When I visited my brother Terry in Hawaii, I watched men's Hula dancing and saw the warrior spirit shine through the dance movements that resemble combat. I was able to see that the fighting arts were hidden and interwoven into the dances and handed down this way for generations. These dances were also codified as a way to teach the fighting techniques in secret when governments banned such activities.

To teach Karate to children, Master Seikichi Toguchi developed several Kata to music. He developed Bo (staff) Kata called "Rhythm Bo". His Shorei-Kan flagship Kata, Hakutsuru No Mai (Dance of the White Crane), is performed to music.

The rhythms of music work nicely when doing Kata. Tempo affects the Kata's timing. Mood affects the feelings of the Kata. Kayo often speaks of doing his Kata to his favorite genre of music, Classical.

Music enhances Kata, helping free the Spirit and allowing emotions to flow.

Karate: Beneath The Surface

I personally had a life changing experience while practicing Kata to music. It changed how I perceived the art, and was the catalyst for me starting this book. I go into detail a bit later on (page 81).

Because Marina is so well versed in music, vocalization, dance and fitness, I asked her to write a passage for inclusion in this book. The following is her insightful contribution. Thank you Marina.

The Art of the Martial Arts

By: Marina Kamen

It starts with your inner voice and lifetime soundtrack. We all connect to times in our lives with certain memories and images in our minds that take us back to a particular activity or place, or reminds us of people we were with. That "feeling" that comes back through us is like a moving motion picture from our past. Who were you when you were young with no inhibitions or pre-expectations?

For many of us, it starts with the music. A sound wave of pitch that surges through our brain and can trigger the most vivid images. These memories may also tap into our bodies and may connect familiar motions and movements. Hearing music can cause a reaction in turn that creates the connection of mind, body and spirit. These three words on their own are often used in a philosophical and out-of-reach way, when really it is all quite simple: Memory, feelings and movement. The natural connection of an action that is a reaction.

Health, fitness, athletics & exercise usually are bottled in a boring package of repetitive and complex movements which is similar to the ever-dreaded "homework assignment". Finding an activity that one likes is harder than it sounds if the only component is the "exercise."

The merger of "feelings" connected to our movements is what takes any "workout" to a completely different level, transforming our bodies and minds collectively. Approaching any form of exercise as an "art form" takes it into the world of "artistry", which requires the connection of the true meaning of threading together "mind, body and spirit".

CHAPTER 4: *CHANGE*

We have all experienced sitting in a doctor's office as they tap just below the knee to check our "reflex". A true physicalization of a reaction to an action. In our lives, we are forever "reacting" to moment-by-moment happenings, 24-hours a day.

Even in our sleep, we react subconsciously to goings on in our lives as our brain takes us on a roller coaster of feelings. A true artist is able to seamlessly weave together a technically trained movement with a true feeling of "reaction" to reach full expression through an art form. Just mimicking a movement and perfecting it through repetition without coming from a true place of feeling and reacting in one's soul is just that – just a movement having nothing to do with the art form.

Our emotions as human beings, being able to easily tap into that inner voice soundtrack and feeling connected to the long term technical trained physical activity is what creates the artistry of the mind, body and spirit connection. If ny one of these three elements missing it dismisses the true artistry of the art form.

Being able to communicate through your art form and move the heart and feelings of others as they observe your creation is the ultimate achievement in artistry.

As in the Martial Arts with styles referring to different animals and pulling movements of style visually, what separates us from the animals, therefore, is the ability to connect mind, body & spirit.

Music, vocalization & dance, in addition to the Martial Arts, all utilize our voice box in addition to our bodies as an instrument. A Kiai utilizes the voice to instill *power* into a movement. Vocalizing on the breath as the power is released is the same as a vocalist who expresses through the voice box supporting it with the center of the body.

Connecting feelings of power, strength, softness with any emotion in order to communicate a feeling is what the term *art form* means. Even when one utilizes the Martial Arts as a fighting art form, the feeling of power, strength, both offensive and defense, must come from a *feeling* in order for the power to be organic and real.

Karate: Beneath The Surface

As many people around the globe train and admire the Martial Arts, one must not forget the true meaning of the term Martial Arts. Why is it not referred to as Martial Exercise, or Martial Defense?

Many of us can remember what it was like to walk into a movie theatre and watch a Martial Arts film, complete with story line, love, war, boy gets girl, etc. The Martial Arts have been utilized to tell stories, and many of the greatest were able to capture the feeling and essence of the art. They were able to communicate a feeling and pull at the heartstrings of the viewer, weaving together through emotion and tapping into our inner voice and senses.

From actor and Martial Artist Bruce Lee to screen-play writer, Robert Mark Kamen whose Karate Kid had us rooting for that young underdog, they did just that. These films utilize the feelings and communication inherent in the Martial Arts, which truly conveys to so many of us the true connection of mind, body and spirit through our innermost feelings.

A New Perspective

My Martial Art was changing.

I was experiencing new feelings while doing Kata. I began exploring different ways to approach them. Then one day, my good friend, fellow Martial Artist and author Gary Gabelhouse introduced me to the concept of Mudra, Mantra and Mandala.

Gary was a long time student of John Roseberry of the Shorei-Kan school in Lincoln, Nebraska. Shihan Roseberry was one of the American GI pioneers who introduced Karate to America. Roseberry was one of the first Americans to study with Toguchi and receive a black belt.

As an explorer, Gary has climbed the highest mountains and trekked through the deepest African jungles. He was exposed to the concept of Mudra, Mantra and Mandala and their relationship to Kata during his own journey to find the elusive enlightenment the Martial Arts promised.

This information changed how I viewed Kata entirely.

CHAPTER 4: *CHANGE*

Mudra, Mantra and Mandala

Indian Yoga practice, the original root of GoJu-Ryu Karate, contains specific body and hand positions, each with its own meaning and use. They are called *Mudra*. The practice requires that a sound is matched to the Mudra. That sound, known as *Mantra* is a spoken word of power.

The Mudra and Mantra are performed through a sequence of dance-like movements creating a three dimensional pattern over time, called a *Mandala*. As the practitioner moves through this pattern he faces benevolent or evil deities, guardians of the entry gate of every section of the Mandala. The practitioner requests permission or crashes through to enter each section using the Mudra and Mantra, until he arrives at the center of the Mandala. Finalizing the dance, he merges with and becomes one with the Mandala.

The purpose of this is to experience an ecstatic feeling. It goes by many names; Awakening, Godliness, Enlightenment, Samadhi, Illuminism, Union or a Religious experience. In other words, a final spiritual state marked by the absence of suffering and the fulfillment of joy.

Karate: Beneath The Surface

In Karate, the Mudra are the physical fighting postures and hand positions contained within the Koryu Kata. The Mantra matched to each technique is the Kiai and the Mandala is the pattern of the Kata, from start to finish. If a 3D video camera could capture the Kata and time-compress it into a single moment, it would be a geometric shape specific to that particular Kata.

Keep in mind, when the Mudra and Mantra are properly executed in Karate, the end result is to maim or kill.

Visual Mandalas are also useful in Karate for meditation and understanding the feeling of a Kata. Each Kata can be represented by various Mandalas. By intently visualizing a specific Mandala for a Kata, a practitioner of the art should be able to experience an emotional and spiritual awakening that the particular Kata invokes.

In summary, I believe that the body position, standing with a straight spine, proper hand positions (Mudra), proper vocalizations (Mantra), synchronized breathing, pattern of movement (Mandala), intense emotional expression and correct spiritual awareness stimulates portions of our brain to produce or suppress neurotransmitters such as dopamine, oxytocin, serotonin, etc., that create ecstatic, religious-like experiences.

This understanding is completely missing in most modern Karate.

Chapter 5: *Preparing The Ground*

Each beginning Karate student is like a seed which grows into a tree that grows in the forest. The forest is like the Dojo where students grow and flourish. Interestingly, Shaolin means, "forest".

Trees begin as seeds that sprout in fertile soil. Before a farmer can plant his seeds and grow his crops, he must first prepare the ground. Often the soil is hard, dry and compact. The farmer must till the soil and make it soft so the seeds can be planted and take root. Survival of the crops require nutrients, so the farmer uses fertilizer to give the young plants what they need. Without this preparatory work, the seeds will not germinate or grow, and the farmer and his family will starve.

In Karate, the seed is the student and the ground is the basic understanding of Kata. Without this preparatory understanding, Kata is just a meaningless dance that accomplishes nothing.

In this chapter I will explore the various ways Kata have been viewed through the ages. Some of these ways have been interwoven into, and taken from, classical Chinese life and religion. Some of these are literal translations of the Kata's name.

And at this chapter's end, I introduce how I view Kata from my newfound experiences, realizations and revelations.

CHAPTER 5: *PREPARING THE GROUND*

What Is Kata

A Kata is a collection of fighting techniques performed in a sequential dance-like order coordinated with specific breathing patterns, following specific directions across the floor. Most Martial Arts include Kata as part of their systems

In the Okinawan system created by Grand Master Chojun Miyagi and further developed by Master Seikichi Toguchi, each Kata has its own theme and each builds upon the foundation of the previous one. In Okinawan GoJu-Ryu Karate there are three types of Kata:

• **Bible Kata**

Sanchin – *Sanchin Kata* was handed down to Higashionna from the White Crane systems of southern China. It is an ancient form designed to build a strong body to withstand strikes, strengthen the internal and external muscles, protect the connective tissues surrounding the muscles, organs and bones, coordinate the breath and body movements, focus the mind, and raise the spirit. Sanchin harmonizes the mind, body and spirit.

Tensho – *Tensho Kata* was created by Miyagi to focus on the soft circular movements missing from Sanchin. It is designed to gather and project power outward through the palms, fingers and feet.

Together, Sanchin and Tensho Kata are considered the Bible Kata of GoJu-Ryu because the entirety of the system is embodied within them.

• **Hookyu Kata:** Training Kata

Miyagi, along with the Shorin schools of Okinawa, designed Gekisai Kata One to become a universally practiced Kata by all Okinawan Karate systems. After Miyagi's death in 1953, Toguchi continued the development of this form to create a complete Kata system that teaches basic and advanced techniques of GoJu-Ryu.

These are considered training Kata, giving the student a well-rounded education in Karate techniques and Kata performance. Each Kata builds upon the previous Kata's techniques. The complete system of Hookyu Kata is as follows:

Hookyu #1
Hookyu #2
Gekisai #1
Gekisai #2
Gekisai #3
Gekiha #1
Gekiha #2
Kakuha #1
Kakuha #2
Hakutsuru No Mai

- **Koryu Kata:** Classical Kata

The Koryu, or Classical Kata of GoJu-Ryu, were either handed down from Higashionna and modified or created by Miyagi. These Kata are based on the Buddhist Sutras and Taoist principles. Advanced fighting techniques and spiritual components are merged in these Kata, as can be seen in the various ancient Mudra.

As the student progresses through these Kata, they can attain a state of Enlightenment, living a fearless and compassionate life.

Saifa
Seiyunchin
Seisan
Seipai
Shisochin
Sanseiru
Kururunfa
Peichurin (Suparinpei)

CHAPTER 5: *PREPARING THE GROUND*

A Kata can be merely fighting. It can also be a blessing or a spiritual exorcism. When you perform a Kata, you are borrowing the Kata temporarily. You are also borrowing the area of practice, and the time of practice. The opening of Kata is performed as a ritual, opening the gate to "the other world". The closing of Kata is just as important, as this ritual closes the gate and keeps the two worlds from interacting. This brings a whole new depth to the concepts of Kata opening - rei (bowing before Kata begins) and yoi (preparatory opening move for all Kata).

Embusen, are lines of direction forming a pattern on the floor. Kata follow embusen. Perpendicular directions signify death while diagonal directions signify life. There is also a vertical component of Kata in the rising and falling of the body. When we practice Kata along the embusen lines, rising and falling and using various Mudra and Mantra, we become the Mandala and are temporarily at one with the spirit world.

Done correctly, that is to say, when the spine is in proper alignment, hands are in the proper position, breath is coordinated, mindset is placed, and emotional content is added, the Go and the Ju unite. Then Kata can bring us to a moment of *Samadhi*, an awakening, a touching of heaven, an ecstasy or a religious experience which is the original purpose of the ancient portions of Kata.

In other words, you become a conduit for many spiritual forces.

There are several basic foundations that Kata are based on. They are translated names, numbers, animals, and elements.

In this book, I will add two more – *emotions and character building* which are not usually associated with Kata practice, but which I assert are two foundations necessary to the art of Karate.

Kata Names

Each Kata has a different and unique name. The names of the Kata are taken from the Chinese ideograms, which have changed over the years and can be interpreted many ways. Also, it is nearly impossible to apply an English translation that makes any sense in some cases.

Karate: Beneath The Surface

Many people have tried to make sense out of these names, but so much secrecy and camouflage has been applied over the years that the actual "meaning" of a Kata cannot be understood just by its name. Also, the complexity of translating the Chinese language due to cultural, religious, geographic and historic influences adds to the confusion. Therefore, to fully define a Kata by its name would be foolish. Nonetheless, the name assigned to a Kata can give us a clue to the Kata's deeper meaning.

These are the names and generally accepted translated meanings of the Bible Kata and Koryu Kata.

Bible Kata:

Sanchin – Three Battles or Conflicts.
Tensho – Misty Rotating Palms.

Koryu Kata:

Saifa – 10 broken stone, rip and tear, pulverize, annihilate, ultimate destruction

Seiyunchin – Control and suppress, to pull into battle

Seisan – 13

Seipai – 18

Shisochin – Four directions battle or conflicts

Sanseiru – 36

Kururunfa – Holding ground

Peichurin (Suparinpei) – 108

The Kata with numbers are understood to originally be from the Shaolin Temple, following the Sutras of Buddhism. Most interpretations, however, give a more obviously Western slant. Common theories are that the numbers represent the number of techniques in the Kata (Hands) or number of footsteps, stances or foot movements (Steps).

Again, to understand the original meanings of the Kata names would require a time machine to ask the originators of the Kata.

CHAPTER 5: *PREPARING THE GROUND*

Kata By The Numbers

GoJu-Ryu Karate has its roots in both the Shaolin External Arts and the Wudang Internal Arts of Bagua Zhang and Xing Yi. These two distinct sources can also be defined as Buddhist Arts (External) and Taoist Arts (Internal). GoJu has elements of both.

Shaolin's Buddhist Kata are identified by a number taken from the Sutras of Buddhism, not from the number of techniques or footsteps in the Kata. There is a grand scheme to this numbering concerning the numbers three and nine, representing the Buddha (himself), the Dharma (Buddhist teachings) and the Sangha (followers of Buddhism) multiplied by the trinity of mind, body and spirit.

No matter what the number and no matter how high you go, it can always be broken down to the numbers three and nine.

Here is the numerology of the Buddhist Kata of GoJu-Ryu:

Sanchin = 3 (mind, body, spirit);
Seisan = 13 (mind, body, spirit) x (heaven, earth, man) + 4 (directions);
Seipai = 18 (mind, body, spirit) x (heaven, earth, man) x 2 (yin, yang);
Sanseiru = 36 (mind, body, spirit) x (heaven, earth, man) x 4 (directions);
Peichurin (Suparinpei) = 108 (mind, body, spirit) x (heaven, earth, man) x 4 (directions) x 3 (past, present, future).

The highest Kata is Peichurin (Suparunpei) meaning 108. 108 is a significant number in Buddhism. 108 is also reached by multiplying smell, touch, taste, hearing, sight, and consciousness (6) by whether they are painful, pleasant or neutral (3), and then again by whether these are internally generated or externally occurring (2), and yet again by past, present and future (3), finally we get 108 feelings ($6 \times 3 \times 2 \times 3 = 108$).

In Buddhist temples at the end of the year, a bell is rung 108 times to finish the old year and welcome the new one. Each ring of the bell represents one of 108 human passions a person must overcome to achieve Nirvana.

Taoism is also involved with Kata numbering. Taoist cosmology is based on the number 8, which is the basis of the most fundamental and advanced Chinese internal-based Martial Arts. When walking the circle in Bagua, one takes 8 steps per round. There are the 8 palm changes of Bagua. 8 times 8 is 64, which numerically symbolizes all of creation in Bagua. Factor in Yin / Yang (opposites) and you get the highest number in Taoism of 128.

A Kata or palm change in a Taoist art dedicates a technique, or series of techniques to all of Taoist creation. In essence the Kata is a physical and spiritual offering. The form symbolizes the world and lives of it adherents. Therefore it must include 8's, for there are 8 elements of reality. The numbers don't relate to the Kata. The Kata relates to the numbers.

Take note: There are 8 Koryu Kata in GoJu-Ryu.

Kata and the Five Elements

In addition to the Yin / Yang theory, Taoist also have the "Five Elements" theory describing the basic interactive nature of the world. The Five Elements are Fire, Earth, Metal, Water and Wood. Each Element has its own attributes. When applied to Martial Arts, each Element is generally applied to individual techniques, but can also be applied to the feelings of a Kata. Under the Five Element theory, there are many factors that will designate one or more of the Elements to a Kata such as time of day, season or even direction you are facing.

The following is a brief introduction to the Five Elements:

Wood is a Yang element. Its main attribute is flexible strength. It also has qualities of generosity, idealism and leadership. The Wood Element seeks to grow and expand, like a tree. Wood represents the start of life, springtime and sensuality. The body parts associated are the liver, gall bladder, eyes, tendons, muscles, nails and nerves. Also associated with the Wood Element are positive feelings of patience and altruism and negative feelings of anger.

Chapter 5: Preparing The Ground

Fire is a Yang element whose energy expands upward and outward. The Fire Element is associated with dynamism, strength and persistence. It symbolizes warmth, enthusiasm and creativity. However, while The Fire Element provides heat and warmth, too much of it can burn painfully, create aggression, impatience and impulsiveness. The body parts associated with the Fire Element are the heart, small intestine, tongue and blood vessels. Happiness is its positive emotion. Hate is its negative emotion.

Earth contains equal portions of Yin and Yang. Its energy is a stabilizing force. The Earth Element is associated with patience, thoughtfulness and hard work. It symbolizes, nurturing, harmony, rootedness, stability, and responsibility. It also includes qualities of ambition, stubbornness and selfishness. The body parts associated with the Earth Element are the spleen, stomach, mouth, flesh and muscles. The positive emotion of The Earth Element is empathy and the negative emotion is worry.

Metal is a Yin element. Its energy pulls inwardly, contracting. Metal represents minerals, crystals and gems. It describes the greatness in each of us. The qualities associated with metal are unyieldingness, rigidity, persistence, strength and determination. The body parts associated with the Metal Element are the lungs, large intestine, bladder, nose, skin and hair. The positive emotion is courage and the negative emotion is grief.

Water is a Yin element. Its energy is downward and its motion is stillness and conserving. The Water Element represents intelligence and wisdom, flexibility and softness. Water can be calm and soothing, yet too much of it can be very powerful and overwhelming. When the Water Element is balanced, you neither hoard nor squander its life giving ability. It also represents a rejuvenating restful state. The body parts associated are the kidneys, bladder, ears, bones, teeth and hair. The positive emotion of the Water Element is calmness and the negative emotion associated is fear.

Kata and the Animals

Through the ages Buddhist and Taoist thought has greatly influenced the Martial Arts of China. Many of the terms used to describe attributes of the Chinese Martial Arts have been coded in a sort of twilight language reflecting unique, physical, and metaphysical characteristics that were exhibited or exemplified by the principles and techniques found within each style. One of the most misunderstood usages of the code words is the 'Five Animals'. The Five Animals are: Dragon, Snake, Tiger, Leopard, and Crane. These five animals' names are code words for deeper meanings.

"Dragon" represents Chi, just like the dragon it cannot be seen, it is forever changing, yet it is powerful and it permeates the universe. The Dragon was believed to cultivate the spirit of the practitioner, and emphasized fluid movement without force or strength.

"Snake" is code for the vicious, brutal, and malicious techniques used in the Martial Arts. The Snake was associated with the cultivation of Chi and personal energy. Snake systems focus on breathing in addition to speed, flexibility and strength.

"Tiger" symbolize fearlessness and an immovable mindset. The Tiger's movements and techniques are hard and aggressive. The Tiger Boxing styles were believed to rely heavily on isometric and isotonic exercises to achieve physical mastery.

"Leopard" much like the Tiger the Leopard signifies strength, swiftness, and resilience. However, the Leopard has more of a guarded nature. But once it takes action it is quicker and more agile than the tiger.

"Crane" stands for power, grace and agile movement. This reflects many facets of a fighter's mentality and strategy. Movements of the crane are associated with swiftness and flexibility. Training with Crane movements is believed to strengthen the body's tendons and ligaments.

There are other animals that have been mimicked in the Martial Arts world: monkey, mantis, turtle and even the gorilla and elephant are some examples.

Chapter 5: Preparing The Ground

Many Martial Artists either misunderstand or they were never taught the correct meaning behind the symbolic code. They spend their lifetime practicing only the technical part of the "Five Animals" and never reach the higher levels of the underlying concepts. Instead of training in the mental and psychological elements, they ignorantly just imitate the movements of the animals. So, instead of learning how to be swift and clever like the monkey, they imitate the monkey's actions such as rolling on the ground, blinking their eyes, scratching their body, while making funny noise; none of which has anything to do with the animal's spirit. They end up looking like clowns instead of Martial Artists.

Kata Fighting Applications

Every technique in each Kata has multiple applications for fighting.

Think of the techniques as a door. The reason the door exists is to separate two spaces and allow passage between them. If we examine the single use of the door, we could say the door is for walking out of a room, or it can be for walking into a room. The door can also be used to prevent entrance or exit with a lock. A door can also be built with the additional purpose to isolate sound, as in my recording studio.

The same applies to all of the martial techniques in a Kata. Each technique has multiple applications and structural design, each dependent on a specific, unique and ever changing purpose.

Kata As An Emotional State

In the Martial Arts we are taught to control and suppress our emotions. It is universally accepted that emotions just get in the way of fighting effectively. But all that changed for me in 2012.

I traveled to visit Chi-I-Do Dojos in two different cities with Kayo. The students in one of the Dojos were hot blooded and passionate. They laughed a lot and their Karate was very powerful. The students in the other Dojo were cool blooded, stiff upper-lip types. They did not laugh much and their Karate was not so strong. It was as if they were stuck in that " circle of shoes" I described earlier. The one that taught me to bottle my emotions as a child.

Karate: Beneath The Surface

This got me thinking; We are Human, and our Martial Arts should express our sentient nature, with all of our wonderfully unique characteristics, one of them being emotions.

Emotions cause us to change the world around us.

Emotions create new life with love and resultant birth. Emotions take away life through rage and resulting death. It is the emotions that drive us to do wonderful things and horrible things to each other. Many believe that Karate should be practiced emotionless. However, let us not forget that Bruce Lee said, "you must fight with emotional content."

The most powerful force of human experience is emotion.

Martial Arts are energy management systems based on the generation, absorption, redirection and projection of physical *and* emotional energy. These energy management systems can be learned through the practice of Kata. One primary purpose of each Kata of GoJu-Ryu is to be a conduit for the projection of physical *and* emotional energy.

Kata is a physical manifestation of an emotional state.

Developing the ability to *infuse* emotional energy into a physical technique can increase the power and effectiveness of that technique. A simple punch thrown as a mechanical movement may be strong, but that same punch thrown with raging anger infused into the punch will do much more damage. An emotion infused punch not only attacks the physical body, but also the psychological, emotional and spiritual energy of the opponent.

The idea is to "turn on" an emotion when you want to use it and then turn it off. And just as with physical techniques where transitional speed is so important – such as a punch following a block – the speed at which you change emotions is paramount.

There is a significant difference between *choosing* to use emotions and not getting or being emotional. Once you master *using* emotions as just another tool in your toolbox of techniques, you will never be controlled by your emotions. You will control them.

CHAPTER 5: *PREPARING THE GROUND*

Kata as physical manifestations of emotional states are as follows:

Sanchin – Unification;
Tensho – Clearing;
Saifa – Rage;
Seiyunchin – Love;
Seisan – Purify;
Seipai – Confidence;
Shisochin – Clarity;
Sanseiru – Projection;
Kururunfa – Joy;
Peichurin (Suparinpei) – Fearless Compassion.

By infusing emotion into Kata as another tool in our toolbox, Kata becomes so much more than a series of forms. Unexpected and wonderful transformations begin to take shape both within the Martial Artist's techniques and in his or her nature, one feeding off the other to complete the circle of training (as in the Yin/Yang circle of life).

Cracking Open with Kururunfa

This was the moment that changed everything for me!

One beautiful summer day, I was walking along the beach listening to Marina's meditative music and practicing movements from Kururunfa Kata. As I practiced, I experienced something *different* during the "full nelson release" section of the Kata.

I had closed my eyes to "feel" the technique. As I rose and opened my palms upward, I felt like I could not get enough air into my lungs. I opened my eyes and was struck by the day's absolute beauty. I was overcome by a feeling of inspiration. It was overwhelming.

As I reached up, I envisioned a dark cloud of suffering hanging over my head. I dug my fingers into it, grabbed it and pulled it to my chest, and then discarded it to the ground. All of my emotions came pouring out of me. I felt rage and love, tension and release.

It was as if everything I had bottled up, released in a violent explosion. I landed on my butt on the sand in tears, experiencing a total emotional breakdown.

As I sat on that beach with my tears streaming down my cheeks, while the waves gently rolled in and out, I realized I had stumbled upon something special and profound. To be sure, I stood up and did it again and again. I was able to repeat the experience each time I performed the sequence. I asked myself, "is this what Kata was supposed to do?"

Upward Hands Raised in Prayer

The origins of Okinawan GoJu-Ryu are from the Shaolin arts which were performed with open hands. However, Chojun Miyagi closed the hands to fists, particularly in the Kata's opening movements. There are no written records about why he chose to do this. Many theories exist to explain it, but no one really knows and therefore virtually all GoJu practitioners use closed fists when opening Kata. Kayo often speaks about the original Chinese way, and many students in our Dojo use the Kata's closed hand opening as seizure and ripping techniques.

CHAPTER 5: *PREPARING THE GROUND*

I began opening my Kata using the double hand "on guard" position with open hands and I could feel the same inspiration as I experienced on the beach. This experience led me to search "upraised hands in prayer" images on the Internet.

I had stumbled upon the ancient hand position that is present in the two Bible and five Koryu Kata of GoJu-Ryu. And this realization and discovery led me to change how I began my Kata.

I no longer moved from ready position with closed fists by my sides to the closed fist double-hand "on guard" position used in our classical Buddhist-based forms, such as Sanchin. I began to open my hands and extend them upwards toward heaven, breathing in deeply, pause for a moment offering my love and gratitude and accepting the gift of knowledge before closing my fists and settling down to the "on guard" position. I found that doing this caused tears to run down my face as I reached up and out. I was blown away.

It is a heavenly feeling.

This was a subtle yet powerful change in my Kata opening which only an experienced Martial Artist's eye could detect. But in Kata, it's the small things that make all the difference. My Karate had suddenly begun to *feel* different.

My perceptions of what Kata was had changed. I began applying emotion into the Kata and saw a pattern. My Kata strengthened and I became more aware of Kata's higher purpose. It was as if the underlying feelings were driving me to an end goal.

This led me to formulate a new theory of Koryu Kata: Each Kata was no longer a stand-alone series of fighting techniques and strategies, but a purposely woven system that had a specific design, a higher emotional purpose layered on top of the physical (martial) and interwoven with the spiritual. This is what I came to perceive as Kata's final goal.

The Kata were becoming connected like stones along a path.

Stepping Stones

While within each individual Kata you can reach a state of ecstasy, taken as a *stepping stone sequence* from Saifa through Peichurin, Kata suddenly transforms into a vehicle to reach enlightenment, a state of fearless compassion and a way of life.

Many will recoil from this concept and many will say I am crazy. I am obviously crazy if my mindset is based on "Karate is fighting" and nothing more. Many will say I don't know what I am talking about; however, they may be trapped by viewing the Kata through their own filters, whether it's fighting, fitness, spirituality or any number of religious perspectives. One experienced Martial Artist sternly warned me to "never speak of this again!" and Kayo said, "I didn't teach you that nor did I ever teach anyone that. This is your idea".

An interesting thought about the stepping stone approach to Kata is *reverse reflection*. Things you learn in one Kata reflect back to previous Kata and enrich them further. This is the learning process for Kata mastery.

You will always see things through your filtered lens unless you can think in new and unexpected ways. You must first "let go" of your preconceived notions of Karate to see it in a new light.

Chapter 6: *Kata*

True realizations that change a person's life are few and far between.

Using the Kata as stepping stones toward a specific goal, rather than simply learning new fighting techniques, is a realization that shook me to my core and changed how I view Karate. This concept is life changing for the Karateka with an open mind and who is open to the endless possibilities that Kata holds.

This is the gem of Kata.

Kata is not just practiced on the Dojo floor. I visualize the Kata throughout my day. I practice the specific hand movements as well. I also ponder the deeper meaning of the Kata and apply the lessons ingrained throughout my daily interaction with others.

Practiced in this manner, life becomes one big Kata.

CHAPTER 6: *KATA*

Opening Kata

The beginning of Kata is a ritual to *open the door* to "the other world" between the living and the dead. We stand at attention, bow and say, "Please teach me," or in Japanese, "onegai shimasu," do an opening salutation with our hands, spread our feet and move our hands to a ready position.

Let's look at this in more detail:

Attention – Press your tongue against the roof of your mouth and slowly breathe in through your nose downward to your lower abdomen (Dantian), then drop your tongue, slowly breathe out of your mouth and focus your attention on your body. Continue to breathe deeply, but softly. Stand with your heels together and toes pointed outward at a 90-degree angle. Stretch your spine upward, pull your chin down and in to keep the back of your neck straight, tuck your hips in and up to keep the lower spine straight and keep your hands open with your fingers pressed together at your side. Place your hands firmly against your outer thigh. Move your hands slightly around and find that one spot that "feels" right. It's hard to describe this spot but you'll know it when you find it. This will help with Chi circulation. Focus on breathing slowly, in through the nose, down into the lower abdomen and back, and out through the mouth. Become aware of your heartbeat and blood circulation. Feel every part of your body as you stand perfectly still.

Then extend your awareness outward. What do you see? What do you hear? What do you smell? What other things in your immediate environment can you sense? Then extend your attention further out, past the walls of your Dojo. What is the season? What time of day? What are the temperature, humidity, and weather conditions? What activity is occurring outside?

You are becoming aware of yourself, your environment and the Universe.

Once you have achieved total awareness, or *mindfulness*, you bow in respect to the teachers who have gone before and say, "Please teach me."

The next movement is to cross the hands in front of your body, tracing the Chi force that surrounds you with your palms while you breathe in deeply into your Dantian and lower back. The left hand covers the right hand, signifying the offer of peace first and war second, as the left hand is connected to your heart-energy signifying compassion.

Next, pivot on the balls of your feet and open your feet to shoulders width apart while you trace your hands back along the circular Chi force. Breathe out as your hands reach the sides of your thighs. Close and squeeze your hands into fists, press downward and bend the energy outward as if it were an iron bar.

Fill yourself with the feeling described for each Kata in the following section. Let the feeling permeate your mind, body and spirit. Throughout the Kata, turn the feelings on and off as the techniques demand. You will learn to control your emotions, never letting your emotions control you.

You are now ready to start Kata.

Closing Kata

The closing sequence of Kata is just as important and perhaps more so than the opening. The purpose of the closing ritual is to *close the door* to "the other world". Seen as a smooth rising of the hands, the movements are actually a double handed Mudra of *fearlessness* followed by a double handed Mudra of *compassion*. These movement are followed by the rising of the hands, with the palms facing you as you breathe in, sucking in the Universal energy.

The next movement is lowering your hands into the beginning position, covering your groin area while you breathe out. The hands are held like two spears with the left hand covering the right. This lowering of the hands movement is actually washing your energy fields (chakras) of the energy you built during the Kata, and sending the power down into the Earth. Trace the Chi energy once again with your hands, placing your palms on the outside of your thighs and take three cleansing breaths.

CHAPTER 6: *KATA*

The final movement is the ending bow reciting "thank you very much," thanking your teacher, your teacher's teachers and all who have gone before you for their help and guidance.

Opening and closing the Kata of GoJu-Ryu is, in a way, a prayer. Always approach your Kata with this in mind.

The Mandalas of Kata

After researching and meditating on thousands of Mandalas, I have chosen ones that represent the feeling and character traits of each Kata – as I experience them. By no means are these the only Mandala you can use for Kata practice and meditation.

Part of the journey of Martial Arts is self discovery. This is my journey, so these are my Kata Mandalas. I advise all Martial Artists to research Mandalas for your own use since the path you travel is yours and yours alone.

I present the following Mandalas as visual representations, along with the emotional intent, character trait, or spiritual power of each Kata.

Pay attention to the geometric shapes contained within the overall pattern, particularly the Yin / Yang symbols, the triangles, the eight chambers and the compass points.

As you stare into these Mandalas, feel the emotions portrayed by the colors and shapes radiating throughout the images.

Visualize these Mandalas and let the images guide you.

****

Please note:

I highly recommend that you thoroughly learn each Kata, including all applications of the techniques contained, before applying any of the following concepts.

Sanchin

Emotional Intent: Unification

Sanchin Kata is the first "Bible" Kata and the basis for all of GoJu-Ryu.

Sanchin is designed to harmonize the mind, body and spirit. It is referred to as "moving Zen". The basic principles and strategies of defense and attack are buried in Sanchin: Rooting, grounding, voiding, deflection, projection, absorption, repelling, ripping, tearing, gouging, locking, breaking and throwing. Sanchin teaches us how to coordinate specific breathing patterns with physical movement, mindfulness and sense of higher spiritual power (the three conflicts of mind, body and spirit). When doing Sanchin, concentrate on the connection between the Dandian, back of the neck and between the eyes.

Sanchin is an emotionally neutral Kata.

Chapter 6: *Kata*

Sanchin is performed with deep, slow breathing into the Dandian and intense dynamic muscle tension, developing a body capable of withstanding powerful blows. This development is called the *iron shirt* or *invisible armor*. Sanchin is considered to be a Go, or hard Kata, but in reality it is a fine balance of hard and soft. Chojun Miyagi said, the goal is to connect and balance all of these elements and reach a state of *"Sanchin ecstasy"*. It is possible that the ecstasy you feel is the result of feel-good chemicals produced in the brain due to the straight spine and arm alignment in coordination with the specific breathing patterns, emotional and spiritual placement within your consciousness.

During the early developmental days of GoJu-Ryu, Chojun Miyagi supposedly required new students practice Sanchin every day for three years before learning any other Kata. Sanchin is necessary to develop a firm understanding of the basics of GoJu-Ryu Karate and a body strong enough to practice the art. While Sanchin may seem to be a simple and easy Kata to perform, it is not. The intense torqueing of the arms and legs coordinated with the deep breathing and body locking makes this Kata very hard to do.

It is the only Kata where the instructor checks the student's strength and body alignment through a ritual called "Sanchin Shime". During Sanchin Shime, the instructor feels the muscle and bone alignment, tests the strength of the body and stance by striking, pushing and pulling various parts of the student's body, and manipulates the student's Chi by projecting or absorbing his own Chi into or out from the student's body. In this ritual, the student suffers pain which he must ignore and endure. This is the heart of the iron body training and the beginnings of learning compassion.

In some cases, instructors who are not properly educated in Sanchin Shime will strike the student too hard in the wrong places or at the wrong times. This is dangerous and must not be tolerated on the Dojo floor. It will cause unnecessary suffering on the student's part and may result in either bodily, emotional or spiritual damage to both student and teacher.

When done properly, Sanchin is a wonderful Kata. If I only have time in my day to do just one Kata, it will be Sanchin.

Tensho

Emotional Intent: Clearing

Tensho is Chojun Miyagi's creation and his answer to the hardness of Sanchin. It means "Misty Rotating Palms". Miyagi developed Tensho based on rotating palm and wrist techniques he learned on his trips to China. Tensho is part two of the Bible of GoJu-Ryu.

Tensho focuses on soft circular hand, wrist and arm movements with coordinated breathing to generate, control and project Chi. It is a Kata of calm control. The key in Tensho is to *let go* of all tension, allowing your energy to flow into your hands and feet, projecting it outwards. A supplementary exercise is moving your hands as if they were fish or lobster tails swimming in water.

Tensho is a clearinghouse of physical and spiritual blockages. The Kata wipes the student's emotional slate clean. It is considered to be a *Ju* or soft Kata but similarly to Sanchin, it is a blend of both hard and soft.

Tensho, like Sanchin, is also an emotionally neutral Kata.

Chapter 6: *Kata*

Too many students misunderstand the relationship of Tensho to Sanchin, and attempt to perform them the same way – with full body tension and loud breathing. The idea in Tensho is to soften the body and perform the techniques with fluid motions, while projecting power into and out of the hands and feet. The breathing in Tensho has more of a lively feeling than the heavy breathing in Sanchin.

If tension is added to the Kata, it is focused to the hands and fingers, maximizing the bending and twisting of the wrists and strengthening of the fingertips. The direct result is the development of strong forearms and fingers facilitating the joint breaks, tearing and ripping we find throughout the GoJu-Ryu Kata.

The hand movements in Tensho, as in all Kata, are combat based, but they can be also interpreted as "gestures to convey a message" or *writing words of power* in space. Keeping this in mind adds yet another layer of spiritual complexity when deciphering this Kata's deeper meaning and purpose.

The key Mudra in Tensho are fearlessness and compassion. The rising, falling and sideways hand movements are also reminiscent of *a religious sign of power*. I don't know if Miyagi had experienced a religious realization during his travels, experimentation or interactions with religious groups on Okinawa but it may be a possibility due to the similarities in the physical motion and spiritual work involved with Tensho.

Much of Miyagi's original intentions are unknown and, therefore, any attempt to nail down the what and why of Tensho is shrouded in mystery.

Perhaps that is the intent of Tensho, to explore the mystery of the misty rotating palms.

Saifa

Emotional Intent: Rage

Saifa Kata is the first Koryu Kata of Traditional Okinawan GoJu-Ryu Karate.

Kayo once told me that in order to build a new and better building, you must first destroy the old one standing in the way… "go practice Saifa".

The word "Saifa" means to break stone 10 times. The purpose of this Kata is to destroy by pounding, pulverizing, smashing and tearing, to destroy and defeat. In essence, Saifa is a violent, destructive Kata.

The base human emotion is rage. This is the first emotion we address in the Koryu Kata, since it is the most destructive and most easily stimulated. Some people lose their temper and quickly become angry. Some people are slow to anger and some even have a very hard time expressing anger at all, avoiding it at all costs. Sometimes a person becomes angry, does not express it but holds onto it for a long time becoming passive aggressive whereas others release their anger quickly.

CHAPTER 6: *KATA*

Use Saifa Kata to practice controlling your feelings of rage. The goal is not to become angry, but rather to use anger as a tool, as you would use a block, punch or kick. The result is to turn your anger on and off at will instantly, infusing its power into the techniques.

A punch thrown with no emotion is not as powerful as a punch thrown infused with rage. It not only contains kinetic force, but spiritual force. Synchronized with the breath, this is your most powerful punch.

When beginning Saifa Kata, fill your mind with the feeling of rage. Picture disturbing events from your life in which you became angry, sad and hurt. Imagine people who have done bad things to you. Think about times you may have been bullied, cheated on, stolen from, abused or beat up. Then, as the anger builds to a peak, dive into the first sequence with full physical and emotional force. That technique completed, stop and let the anger go, and calm down. Then build up the anger again into the next sequence. Release and continue through the Kata this way.

By turning the rage on and off through the Kata, you will gain control of your anger.

At first it will be hard to do. However, as you practice Saifa this way, your Kata will get stronger and you will become proficient at raising the rage quickly and letting it go quickly. The speed of this transition is very important. The faster you can cycle the emotion on and off, the better.

You have now added anger to your Martial Arts toolbox.

Don't let anger control you.
You control the anger.
Use it as needed.

Seiyunchin

Emotional Intent: Love

*Love creates life. Love is the bedrock of compassion.
Love is a very powerful emotion.*

Seiyunchin means to control, suppress, pull off balance, grasp and pull into battle making the enemy fight your fight. You have your opponent completely under control.

If Saifa Kata teaches us how to control and use our rage, never again becoming angry, Seiyunchin teaches about the other end of the emotional spectrum – *love*. If you can convince a potential opponent that he has nothing to fear, he may let down his guard, and allow you to control the situation and get a tactical advantage or hopefully avoid a confrontation.

Seiyunchin primarily moves along the diagonal lines of the embusen signifying life. Also, love is a primary motivator in creating life.

Chapter 6: *Kata*

The body has several energy centers (chakras). The chakra most focused on in Martial Arts is the Dantian. In Seiyunchin we also pay attention to another vital chakra; the heart. We concentrate on *balancing* the heart chakra, located in the center of your chest.

When you begin Seiyunchin Kata, fill yourself with loving thoughts. Think about the people you have affection for, when you got your first job, your first love and your first accomplishments. As these feelings reach a peak, step into the first frame of Seiyunchin. As you perform the Kata, notice that your hands cross the body's centerline. With each hand motion, you actually manipulate the energy around your heart.

During the first three movements your hands open the heart chakra and then offer love to your opponent. The Kata then takes us through several *manipulations* of the heart energy. We project out from, and absorb into, the heart. We rip and tear at it, balance it through vertical movements and turn it over in the double elbow sections. We finish the Kata by holding the heart gently between our hands.

The goal is to infuse peaceful, soft and loving feelings into your technique as you manipulate and project your heart energy.

An observer may even be able to detect a slight smile on your face while doing Seiyunchin Kata.

In addition to the emotional aspect of Seiyunchin, the Kata's physical principles include: Rising and falling, expansion and contraction, synchronization of foot and hand, and build up of power with a sudden explosive release. This Kata has elements from the internal Taoist art of Xing-Yi (Mind-Boxing) mixed with the Shaolin arts.

Several sections of Seiyunchin are performed quite slowly, giving the Kata a meditative quality. Aside from Sanchin, this Kata is the one most likely, in Karate circles, to be categorized as "moving meditation". Contrary to this belief is that while moving slowly in Seiyunchin, you are generating intense, but controlled, emotional and physical energy.

Being able to control our emotions is vital in the Martial Arts. Saifa and Seiyunchin Kata are designed to teach that important lesson.

Seisan

Emotional Intent: Purify

Seisan is the first of the Buddhist numbered Kata (13) after Sanchin.

The opening of the Kata is a double-handed, closed-fist, chest block. But if you open your hands, they are in the same position most religions of the world use to pray. With hands raised you give your love and ask for grace from whatever you believe to be a higher spiritual power. Opening Seisan this way gives us a feeling of sanctification, purification and a connection to the universal powers underlying everything we do.

Throughout the various Mudras in Seisan Kata, you can feel a sense of a higher power and purpose. The Mudras connect heaven, man and earth through rising palms, forward palms and downward palms in various combinations.

Seisan Kata multiplies the three conflicts of mind, body and spirit, by the connection of heaven, man and earth plus the four directions – north, south, east and west – in which the Kata is performed gives Seisan its Buddhist number of thirteen: 3 x 3 + 4 = 13.

Chapter 6: *Kata*

Interestingly, the four compass directions signify death (whereas the four diagonals signify life). I find this interesting because when we enter the Dojo we consider ourselves dead, and when we leave we are given the gift of life once again. In other words, upon entering the Dojo we face our death in possible combat and strive to purify our spirit by training in the space between the worlds of the living and the dead.

Performing Seisan Kata should feel like a religious prayer. This is why opening the hands and pausing slightly upon the opening double chest blocks is important. As you open, breathe in deeply and fill yourself with the universal energy. Absorb the energies of the students surrounding you. Suck it all in and sink it into your Dantian. This way of approaching Seisan will give your opening three punches tremendous spiritual power that will sustain through to the end of the Kata.

Seisan is a powerful Kata meant to fight hand-to-hand against other *unarmed* people. Like Sanchin Kata, Seisan contains virtually everything one would need in a non-weapon altercation. The Kata is designed for in-close fighting with short range, powerful yet simple techniques.

Historically, Seisan Kata is a direct descendant of the Luohan Quan Buddha Palm; the root style that most Shaolin Kung Fu and many other non-Shaolin styles are based on. It was handed down by the Buddhist monks who escaped Shaolin's destruction.

There are many versions of Seisan Kata practiced by different Karate styles. The GoJu-Ryu version is a simplified one containing the core and main principles of the original Shaolin form, complete with the ancient Mudras.

Purifying ourselves through Seisan Kata clears the way for us to move from an emotional space to a character building practice as we will see in the next Kata, Seipai.

Seipai

Emotional Intent: Confidence

Previously we learned to control our emotions with Saifa and Seiyunchin and purified ourselves through the sanctification of Seisan.

Next we start building confidence through Seipai Kata.

Seipai Kata is a Buddhist form originating from the Shaolin Temple combined with circular elements of the Internal Taoist art of Bagua.

Interestingly, while Seipai is a Buddhist form, the first three sequences are not done the same way as the other Buddhist forms of Sanchin, Seisan, Sanseiru and Peichurin (Suparumpei) – with a double chest block/punch sequence. Although, upon closer examination, the opening right knife hand parry of Seipai is just a variation of a closed hand chest block and the next two movements combining chest blocks and punches are just like in the other Buddhist Kata. Look closely and you will see the chest block and punch. The difference is the hands are clasping each other rather than apart. It is another variation on a theme.

Chapter 6: *Kata*

Seipai means eighteen (18) which is the product of the unification of mind, body and spirit (3) multiplied by heaven, earth and man (3) encompassing the duality of Yin and Yang (2). This Kata primarily utilizes circular and evading techniques while advancing toward your opponent. It contains energy redirects, joint breaks and throws.

While Saifa, Seiyunchin and Seisan Kata all involve fighting against the unarmed opponent, Seipai Kata is designed to fight against an opponent armed with a mid to long range bladed weapon such as a spear, sword or knife.

Facing a bladed weapon requires a different mindset and strategy from facing an unarmed opponent. You cannot retreat while blocking the weapon since the tip of the blade will chase you down and cut you to ribbons. You must sidestep into the attack creating a void then counter with a disarming and finishing technique such as a limb or neck break.

Seipai is aggressive in nature and it teaches us how to close the gap between an opponent several feet away while avoiding his long-reaching blade, disarming and defeating him. The only way to prevent getting cut is to move forward with *extreme confidence* in yourself and your techniques.

The opening posture, as well as several others in Seipai Kata, will give you a sense of confidence and self-assurance. When moving into and holding these postures, keep confidence in your mind and take command of the floor.

I cannot stress how important having confidence is in life and especially in Seipai.

As you move into the higher Kata, confidence is required. You will be facing more difficult challenges, in the physical, emotional and spiritual sense. Your fortitude will be tested.

Shisochin

Emotional Intent: Clarity

After we have built our confidence through Seipai, the next step up the ladder is to rid ourselves of any doubts, or delusions. We do this with Shisochin Kata, meaning four corner conflict or battle.

Shisochin Kata is related to Seiyunchin Kata. Miyagi may have formulated these Kata based on his experiences with Xing-YI Quan, a Taoist internal Martial Art meaning, "mind boxing".

As in Seiyunchin, the basic physical principles of Shisochin are: Rising and falling, expansion and contraction, synchronization of foot and hand, and build-up of power with a sudden explosive release.

The drop elbow sequences are straight out of a Chi-Gung handbook for power development..

Chapter 6: *Kata*

But the key to Shisochin is the Mudra, a swiping block followed by an arm break or throw. This movement, in terms of Mudra, means to *wipe away all delusion* with the *Sword of Enlightenment*. Imagine the movement as drawing open a curtain, which has shielded, masked or distorted the true nature of things. This Mudra is performed in the four diagonal directions, signifying life, for total clarity of reality.

Delusion is an idiosyncratic belief or impression that is firmly maintained, despite being contradicted by reality, or rational deduction.

Shisochin Kata deals with ending delusion

We all have preconceived notions about ourselves and the world. Most of our beliefs have been shaped through our own filters and the perceptions of those around us. Unfortunately, our views of reality often substantially differ from *actual* reality. Things aren't always what they appear to be. Often the truth is masked in response to inner turmoil, lack of confidence, jealousy, insecurity, etc.

Karate is not just about fighting. It is also about living with other people. In order to interact mindfully, we must be able to see through other people's self-created images (or delusions) they build around themselves.

As we move on to the next Kata and reach higher spiritual planes, we need to see the world and ourselves clearly, without distortion.

Do not doubt your techniques and ability. Strive to see the world as it truly is – not through your predefined filters. Strive to know your true self without ego getting in the way. Cut through the delusion and see clearly.

The ability to see reality clearly is a fundamental stepping stone on the path towards enlightenment.

Wipe away all doubt and delusion with Shisochin Kata.

Sanseiru

Emotional Intent: Projection

So far in our Kata journey, we have mastered our emotions with Saifa and Seiyunchin, achieved purity through Seisan, gained confidence in Seipai and achieved clarity by wiping away any remaining doubts or delusion with Shisochin. We are now ready to leave the Dojo, and *project* ourselves out into the living world.

Sanseiru is the next Buddhist based Kata. We arrive at Sanseiru's meaning of *thirty six* by multiplying the *nine* of Seisan (mind, body and spirit x heaven, earth and man) by the *four* compass points (north, east, south, west).

While the previous Kata teach fighting against man, Sanseiru Kata works on the spiritual plain of *psychic projection*. The four perpendicular compass point directions of the Kata signify death. The danger of doing Sanseiru lies in the connection of death and psychic projection. If you do not end the Kata properly, closing the door between the two worlds of the living and the dead, strange and unpleasant things may occur in your life. In Sanseiru you are, in essence, battling death. This Kata must be trained under the supervision of an advanced teacher.

CHAPTER 6: *KATA*

Sanseiru Kata teaches how to project yourself into the world.

The techniques in Sanseiru Kata are done with a feeling of "reaching out and touching someone". The double kick and following kick elbow sequences, as well as the double block into double punch, teach us to shoot our powers out in all directions.

Through Sanseiru Kata, and the focus on projecting outwards, we examine how others perceive us; who we are, and what we have in our lives.

How you dress, wear your hair, walk, talk, act and how you interact with others is the spiritual key to Sanseiru Kata. Look at the achievements. Look at your failures. Look at your family and friends, your work and hobbies, your health. Equally important, is how others feel about us and the actions we take.

You can see how you project yourself out into the world by looking at the results of your projection. Do people like you or are they afraid? Are others attracted or repulsed by you? What kind of life do you have?

There are people who change the world for the better through their projection, those who make almost no difference and those who cause destruction and pain.

After learning Sanseiru from Kayo, I began imagining fights everywhere I went. Getting into fights was the last thing I wanted and I knew if I kept on that course, I would attract the very thing I did not want. I also began to notice, in the Dojo, that junior students were reacting to my "projecting" at them during two person drills. They were passing out *before* I even touched them. It freaked me out and I stopped training at the Dojo for several years. I used the time to understand that in order to reach enlightenment through the Martial Arts my techniques *had* to be deadly, but, moreover, that *intent* needed to be *projected*.

People perceive and react to who you are, based on your projection. So take a good look at your life, and if you don't like what you see, change it. Project yourself out into the world, the way you want, and live life to it's fullest. Sanseiru Kata will give you that ability.

Kururunfa
Emotional Intent: Joy

Kururunfa Kata is related to Saifa Kata. Whereas Saifa focuses on the emotion of rage, Kururunfa focuses on eradicating the *results* of rage; suffering.

Once we learn to project ourselves into the world through Sanseiru, we look around through the clarity of Shisochin and see how much *suffering* there is in the world. Every one of us has suffered sometime in our lives. For many, this suffering is constant and debilitating. For others, it is the driving force behind destructive actions that hurt others.

Suffering is like having a dark cloud hanging over your head affecting every aspect of your life.

> *Besides the advanced fighting techniques*
> *contained in Kururunfa Kata,*
> *it is also designed to end suffering*
> *resulting in a joyful life.*

Chapter 6: *Kata*

Kurununfa Kata's opening contains movements that stretch the hip joints, since this Kata relies on hip torqueing to achieve maximum power. The sequences in Kururunfa build your Chi by driving forward, projecting power from the Dantian and building to climactic explosions.

The animal most referred to for Kururunfa is the Dragon. The Dragon is powerful and wise yet remains hidden and unseen. It has tremendous patience and will wait eons to emerge. When it does, it comes forth with its whipping tail, fire breath and tremendous strength. Many of the techniques in Kururunfa mirror these qualities of "holding and striking suddenly".

The "full nelson release" sequence is the spiritual heart and center of the Kata, and involves raising your hands in joyous prayer, then reaching into that dark cloud of *suffering* hanging over your head, yanking it down (Kiai is "Ha") and discarding it by tossing it into the ground (Kiai is "Hey").

It is a spiritual cleansing of the highest magnitude.

The first time you do this properly, as you drop to the ground, you will be overcome with sadness. This is your body processing the *suffering*, converting it to Chi in your Dantian, and then dissipating it by throwing it away, into the ground. It is an extremely powerful movement.

When I first discovered this, I found myself sitting on my butt in the sand at the beach, sobbing uncontrollably. It felt as if all my troubles were suddenly lifted off my shoulders. All that was left was the deep blue sky, lightly lapping waves, a slight breeze in the air and a feeling of wonder and absolute joy. It was a watershed moment in my Martial Arts training and profoundly changed my experience of GoJu-Ryu Kata.

Kururunfa means "to hold ground". Perhaps the spiritual interpretation of this is to stand firm against the suffering of mankind, defeat it and release the joy that springs forth from the universe.

This is a powerful Kata that paves the way and prepares you for the final and ultimate Kata of GoJu-Ryu, Peichurin.

Peichurin

Emotional Intent: Fearless Compassion

Peichurin (Suparunpei) Kata is the highest form in the Buddhist Martial Arts and specifically GoJu-Ryu. On the first day of the New Year, Buddhists ring a bell 108 times to rid themselves of the 108 *passions of man*. 108 is a meaningful number in Buddhism, and is applied to this Kata.

The foot patterns of Peichurin Kata follow the eight compass points signifying both life and death. The primary hand positions in Peichurin are Abhaya & Varada Mudra, meaning "I am not afraid of you so therefore I can be compassionate to you – I do not fear you, so I can give freely". Servicing others is the highest form of human interaction.

In Peichurin you will face all 108 passions, or emotions, as you move from gate to gate of the Mandala. You use the correct Mudra and Mantra, to request entrance or crash through each gate, merging with the deity guarding the gate. Finally, you enter the heart of the Mandala and become one with the Kata.

Chapter 6: *Kata*

Practicing Peichurin, with these thoughts in mind, will elevate you beyond "skin and bones" Karate and the simple fighting that the Martial Arts have developed into today. It is the Martial Arts of the *enlightened* person, who seeks to make the world around him a better place, free from *suffering* and full of *joy*.

As you walk through the world projecting who you are, no longer subject to your own emotions, delusions and suffering, you walk the path of *loving kindness* based on *fearless compassion*.

This is the purpose and end goal of studying the Kata of GoJu-Ryu.

"I do not fear you. I have compassion for you."

Grand Buddha at Mount Lingshan, China
Expressing the Abhaya & Varada Mudra

Applying Emotion in Kata

One day in the Dojo there was a normally cheery teen green belt who seemed very upset. I knew she had been experiencing heartbreak in her life and I sensed her projecting what seemed like a dark cloud hanging over her head.

I directed her to an open section of the Dojo floor and had her begin Saifa Kata. I instructed her to do the Kata with *anger*. By the third sequence, she burst into tears and almost collapsed. I held her up and told her to keep going. The angrier she got, the stronger her Kata became.

Then I had her switch to Seiyunchin Kata and told her to think of those who loved her. She immediately started crying again throughout the Kata. By the end of class, her Kata was flowing beautifully and her tears had finished falling.

She later told me it was the most powerful experience she ever had and took her quite by surprise. She *felt* so much emotion during Kata practice.

For me this experience was very powerful. I lost awareness of the rest of the Dojo and just focused on her emotional transference to the physical for release. It was intense.

This coupled with my own personal experiences, suggests the possibility of treating a spectrum of psychological issues by adding emotions into Karate Kata training.

Chapter 7: *Compassion*

We've explored infusing our emotions into our Kata and building our character through many years of hard work.

The stepping stones of Kata lead us down the path of becoming fearless and compassionate, but...

What is compassion?

As Martial Artists we have the power to control and harm others. Studying the arts imparts a responsibility upon us to act in the best interests of those whom we live, work and interact with.

How does compassion manifest in the real world? Is it something definable, or is it just an intangible concept held up by the righteous as a badge of honor?

What does compassion look like?

CHAPTER 7: COMPASSION

Things Are The Way They Are

*Things are the way they are,
because that is how they are supposed to be.
If they were meant to be some other way, they would be.*

Life is a series of events that lead to other events in an ever-changing universal drama spanning all of time and existence. Every action has a reaction, in a never-ending chain of events. It's called The Butterfly Effect; that the world is as it is because a butterfly flapped its wings a certain way millions of years ago. If it had not flapped those wings that certain way, everything today would be different.

How does this equate to our lives today, and what does this have to do with Karate?

When I turned thirty, my life was pretty good. My career as a recording engineer was in full swing. Although the Shorei-Kan Representative had betrayed me and my fellow students, my own school in Queens was thriving. I was dating three women, living with my best friend, had my own car and having the time of my life.

Then on one fateful day, my student said, "Hey, there is a guy teaching the same Karate stuff we do at a studio I take dance class at." Following my curiosity, and perhaps Karma, I met Kayo, and here I am today writing this book about Kata and life.

Then, on another day of destiny, Marina stepped into my life. I asked her to marry me two weeks later, and here I am with a long-term marriage to a woman I love, with three amazing children, a successful business and living a wonder-filled life.

Things are the way they are because that is how they are supposed to be. If you don't like something in your life, do something about it and change it. It's as simple as getting up and doing Kata.

Is it hard to do?

You bet it is, but if it were easy, everybody would do it. Unfortunately, most people take the easy way out and let life's events just happen to them. They question why they have no money, a crappy job, a broken family and no aspirations. They end up sabotaging their own efforts at bettering themselves and improving their life experience.

We who practice Martial Arts, learn that striving for self-improvement is hard work. We learn to take a proactive stance in life; we train our Kata so we can become fearless and compassionate in order to make our world the way we want it to be.

*If you don't like something about your life,
do something about it,
and change it.*

The Killer Monks of Shaolin

Killing is not permitted in Buddhism. So how did the Buddhist priests of the Shaolin Temple justify killing using their Martial Arts? This is purely conjecture on my part... It's simple – they were fearless and compassionate. They were acutely aware that people harmed one another due to suffering they had endured sometime in their lives. Suffering is a root of dysfunction in humans. As we learned through Kururunfa, ending suffering is a key component in the journey to enlightenment. Reincarnation is a key belief in Buddhism, so by ending someone's suffering, by ending their life, thereby allowing them another chance in the next life, the priests were practicing the highest level of compassion.

CHAPTER 7: COMPASSION

Fearless Compassion

The goal in studying and practicing the Kata of Okinawan GoJu-Ryu Karate is to become a person who is fearless and compassionate. What does this mean in everyday life?

The highest form of human interaction is selflessly serving others. We offer our kindness to those in need, and help those who are less fortunate.

By following the path of the Kata of GoJu-Ryu, we learn to defend ourselves to the point of becoming fearless. We suffered and no longer fear the pain and struggle of rigorous training. We no longer are afraid of failure or ridicule. We no longer need to fight, because we exude confidence, we radiate power, and we are trained to recognize danger ahead and to avoid confrontation. And we are joyfull.

The most advanced Martial Artist will never be confronted by aggression, because we are trained to control our environment and personal experience.

To be fearless in the face of danger or adversity is of great value, and we Martial Artists strive to reach this point of proficiency in the art, through our practice of Kata. Once fully trained, we avoid danger and adversity. We don't manifest it and we go with the natural flow of a peaceful life.

By living a life of compassion, we create a safe-haven for weaker untrained people. Think of yourself as that great oak tree with roots running deep and wide, stabilizing the soil for all the young saplings struggling to survive in the forest. Imagine your branches reaching to the heavens in a growing canopy of protection for future generations.

To live fearlessly and compassionately helps everyone around us grow and develop healthy emotional resilience. It is the root of great societies, and the great hope that we as teachers strive for in our students.

What Does Compassion Look Like

Throwing around words like fearlessness and compassion is easy. Being fearless and compassionate, and translating that into action, is another thing. So what does being fearless and compassionate look like?

We first study the Martial Arts to learn how to defend ourselves. Once we have mastered physical self-defense, we should be able to walk a life unafraid of others whether physical, emotional or spiritual. We have steeled ourselves against incoming physical attacks, strengthened our moral code and insulated our souls from evil intent. This gives us the freedom to be who we are, unafraid to speak our minds and able to offer ourselves fully and without reservation to help others.

We all have needs. Being compassionate means you can help fill the needs of others without taking anything away from yourself. It requires empathy – the ability to feel what it's like to walk in someone else's shoes. Sometimes, compassion is just listening to a friend who needs to talk. Sometimes it is giving a hungry person something to eat, helping a blind person cross a busy street, or saving an abused animal. Compassion in the Dojo is helping a junior student understand a technique without hurting him, and without becoming frustrated at his inability to comprehend something we understand so well. Compassion is giving of ourselves, without expecting anything in return.

> *When you act compassionately, you do not take.*
> *You do not expect praise for giving.*
> *You give, simply to help others,*
> *because they are in need.*

I am quite aware that we do not live in a perfect world, so does compassion have its limits? A possible issue with giving freely is the possibility of being taken advantage of. Too often, the saying "no good deed goes unpunished" is proven true.

CHAPTER 7: *COMPASSION*

Personal Compassion

In a way, it is easy to have compassion for others. Once you can see things clearly for what they really are, and understand that people's bad behavior is rooted in their own suffering, the path to extending compassion is clear.

What happens when you extend that compassion repeatedly, and the person not only refuses to acknowledge your kind offer, but turns on you and frames your compassion as an attack? And what happens when this occurs repeatedly, as you continue to extend your compassion? Is there an end to your offerings? Does offering compassion have its limits?

When offering compassion leads to your own suffering, then what?

This is a time of self-reflection. It is a time to look inward and offer that compassion to yourself. Life is too short. I am not under any delusion that at my age in my 60's, what is ahead for me and my life is less than what is behind. I have no time to give to those who do not see my compassion for what it truly is, a gift. I can get back my money. I cannot get back my time.

I refuse to end offering compassion to those who are worthy of it because my compassion has worth, as does my desire to extend it. As a rare diamond is pulled from the earth, so is my compassion offered from my soul. It is the ultimate expression of human relationships, not something to be trampled on, to be scorned or shunned. It is to be cherished and celebrated.

There are moments you must look inward and be compassionate to yourself. Get rid of toxic people who take from you what they can, and give nothing in return. Save your compassion for those who are worthy, and can learn and grow using it as spiritual nourishment. Be compassionate to yourself; for you are the source of your compassion and you are worth it!

Betrayal

When people show you who they truly are, believe them!

I have known betrayal up close and personal. It is one of the worst things you can do to another person, and it can test anyone's ability to be compassionate. Betrayal is almost always perpetrated by those closest to you; the ones you trust the most. It cuts like a knife driven deep into the heart. Recovery is extremely hard, and sometimes impossible.

Follow the path you have chosen with all of your being. Keep the Martial Virtues close to your heart and always be true to yourself. Know who is deserving of your love, affection and compassion. Pass on "The Way" to others who prove worthy.

Always be loyal to those who support you and depend on you. Never betray them or your beliefs. Betrayal is a deadly attack on the spirit by those closest to you. It is a stab in the back by one who is trusted to protect your back.

Do not betray those you love; for they have trusted you with their love. Do not betray your teacher; for he has entrusted you with his knowledge. Do not betray your students; for they have given you their loyalty.

Do not betray yourself; for you have chosen to follow the path of a Martial Artist. A Martial Artist who uses his power for good will be one at peace in his mind, body and spirit, and with all of the Universe.

Abuse

GoJu-Ryu founder Grandmaster Chojun Miyagi said, "never strike anyone, and let no one strike you." Unfortunately, there are people who do take advantage of and abuse others. It happens in many relationships.

Marina and I work with The Rachel Coalition, a not-for-profit organization bringing awareness to domestic violence. When I look into the eyes of abuse survivors, I see the pain they've endured. I see the shame they feel. It is heartbreaking to know they have suffered abuse at the hands of people they know, love and trusted.

Chapter 7: Compassion

Abuse takes many forms: domestic, child, work place and bullying are just a few examples of abuse. Remarkably, statistics show that one in three girls, and one in six boys are victims of childhood sexual abuse. While the physical scars often fade with time, the emotional damage lasts a lifetime.

These are common symptoms in survivors of abuse:

> *Chronic pain, gastrointestinal symptoms/distress, musculoskeletal complaints, obesity, eating disorders, sleep disorders, pseudocyesis, respiratory ailments, addiction, chronic headache, psychological and behavioral presentations, depression and anxiety, post traumatic stress disorder symptoms, dissociative states, repeated self-injury, suicide attempts, lying, stealing, truancy, running away, poor contraceptive practices, compulsive sexual behaviors, sexual dysfunction, infidelity, somatizing disorders, poor adherence to medical recommendations, intolerance of or constant search for intimacy, expectation of early death.*

The list just goes on and on. I bring this up, because I believe it is one of the most pervasive problems affecting millions of lives everyday, mostly without any outward physical sign. Abuse is a horror that occurs much too frequently, and almost always behind closed doors. It is a behavior that we must stop whenever we become aware of it. Abuse is the root cause of suffering and shame that destroys lives. It is passed down from generation to generation. The chain of abuse can be stopped, through self compassion and compassion for others. Compassion is the antidote for abuse, shame and suffering.

We learn about abuse and suffering in the Dojo through strenuous training. The workouts are hard, but we overcome the challenges and, over time, develop compassion for ourselves and each other.

Martial Arts vs. Marital Arts

And while on the subject of abuse, I'd like to look at the effect of sexual relations and the opportunity for abuse in the Dojo.

The practice of Martial Arts stimulates our sexual nature. Our bodies become strong and virile, our minds become sharp and our feelings amplify. The natural flow of our nature comes forth in both our Kata and in our sexual performance. It is said that the only difference between Martial Arts and Marital Arts is the placement of the letter "i". The nature of fighting has not changed in millennia and neither has the sexual interaction between men and women. It is natural instinct to both fight and procreate. We do not need to be taught how to do either.

Until recent times, women were not permitted in the Martial Arts training halls. In modern times, however, it is quite common for women to train with men. This is not a problem, until it becomes one.

So it goes in the Dojo. A junior female student is drawn to a senior man, and they begin a relationship. Soon jealousy, from other students or seniors, rises and interferes with the smooth functioning of the Dojo. I have heard stories of teachers having sex with their students' girlfriends on the Dojo floor, under the sacred shrine. I have seen teachers let their girlfriends tell the Dojo seniors what to do, because of their special relationship, and in the process destroy the Dojo; organization leaders trade sex for advanced belts; seniors fight each other for the affections of female students; male students begin sexual relationships with their female counterparts, only to see them break up, and one or both leave the Dojo and stop training. I have heard stories of heads of organizations impregnating their students, and leaving them on their own to suffer the consequences. The knife also cuts in both directions where females become sexually aggressive toward male students. This abuse occurs in same sex interactions as well. The potential for poor, even tragic, outcomes is real and inter-Dojo relationships should be avoided.

Bottom line is that sex and Martial Arts do not go together, no matter how strongly people feel about each other, or their own primal feelings and urges. It is our responsibility to resist the temptation.

Chapter 8: *The Peace Within*

> *Studying Karate is a lifelong endeavor.*
>
> *It is a way of life; a way of seeing and interacting with the world around you, and the universe you inhabit. It has changed me for the better, and has given me the tools I needed to construct a happy and satisfying life.*
>
> *I am certain that if my grandparents saw me today, with the family and life I have, they would be ecstatic with what I have accomplished, and the moral compass I have chosen to follow.*
>
> *My father once told me that all he wished for was for me to make him proud. I know, that as he looks down on me from heaven, he is smiling from ear to ear because I have made good on his final wish.*

Chapter 8: The Peace Within

Balancing The Triad of Life

A well-balanced life is one in which family, career and Martial Arts are carefully honed and intertwine without any stress. Where each part of one's life flows into the other in a harmonious, synergistic circle.

Think of the triad as your stance in life. Putting too much energy into one aspect, your Martial Arts for instance, could potentially destabilize your career or home life much the same as overweighting one leg would leave you prone to being knocked off your stance and thrown. Moreover, when your center is off, neither your blocks nor your attacks will have maximum effect. Quite likely, in fact, your block will turn into an advantage for your opponent because in fending off the attack you're apt to teeter or fall.

To be fully actualized as a Martial Artist one must live a full and balanced life. Family, friends, and career success all feed the spirit thus allowing the Martial Artist to blend the elements of his power: physical conditioning, mental acuity, mindfulness, compassion and humanity to maximum effect.

This is the point of viewing Kata as emotional and character building stepping stones beginning with Sanchin Kata, harmonizing the mind, body and spirit, and ending with the fearless compassion of Peichurin

Healing

In Karate, we are taught to destroy the body, mind, and spirit of our opponent. Equally important, is the ability to heal ourselves. While Western medicine is focused on healing illness, Eastern medicine is focused on preventing illness.

To this end, the Taisho Daruma exercise was developed from the ancient Indian Yogic movements combined with advanced Kata techniques. Taisho Daruma works the body from the toes to the head, stretching and strengthening the muscles, tendons, ligaments and bones.

The specialized breathing methods massage the internal organs, and bathe the body in oxygen flushing out impurities.

The Kata themselves have healing techniques woven seamlessly into the movements. For instance; The opening of Kururunfa Kata is a series of hand blocks, parries, attacks and holds while simultaneously blocking with the leg, and side kicking. This technique can also be used to stretch the hip joint by standing on one leg, holding the ankle with one hand and pressing the knee in various positions with the other elbow.

Done slowly, all Kata can be performed as stretches and isometric exercises. By targeting the breath and chi, you can heal various injuries in the body. Using the *stepping stone* approach to Kata, you can also heal and strengthen your emotional and spiritual health.

Love What You Do

In the quest for healing and creating a good life, I always say "love what you do, don't do what you love". Why? It's simple. If all you do are things you love, and you do them repeatedly with no change, you will soon tire of doing them, until you look for something new and start the cycle again. But if you love what you do, it doesn't matter what it is you do, you will never tire of doing it. Doing only what you love is selfish and shortsighted. It can cut you off from experiencing new things in life.

Love what you do. You'll be happier.

You may ask, "How does this work with Kata that I do over and over again? Doing Kata is something I love to do. Following what you are saying, won't I become bored?"

While it is important to do your Kata repeatedly, don't just do them blindly. You should be learning each and every time you do them. The Kata should always be different even though it may *look* the same, it should not *feel* the same. Your Kata should mature with each repetition. And besides, you should love what you do no matter what it is.

If you follow the Mantra of "love what you do"
you will lead a happy and fulfilled life.

CHAPTER 8: THE PEACE WITHIN

Forgiveness

Marina works on countless fitness television productions. She guides overweight people through fitness programs using her motivational music and positive reinforcement.

These people are not happy with who they are. They focus on their physical or emotional issues and expend great amounts of energy beating themselves up. This thought process blocks them from bettering their lives. Self-hatred drives these people to over-eat and generally treat themselves terribly. So, Marina pays particular attention to the concept of *forgiveness*. One of the keys to Marina's success, is her ability to create a nurturing environment where they can *forgive themselves*.

These people watch what they eat with portion-control and they exercise daily. Everyone loses weight; many over 20 pounds. They all look and feel better than they have in years, if not their entire lives. It is inspirational to watch these folks' transformations.

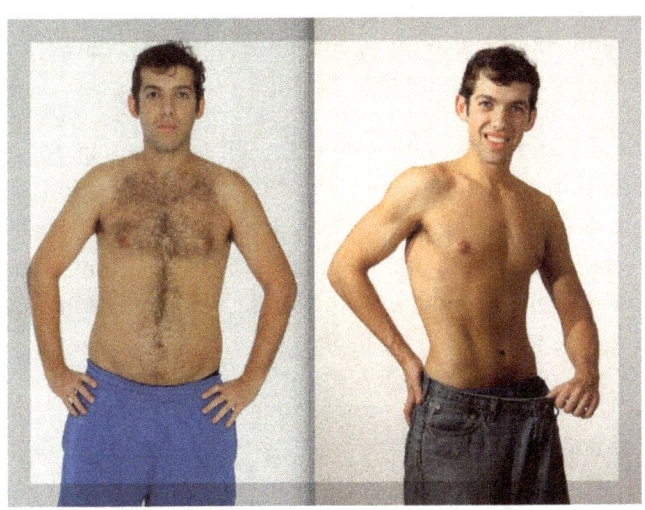

I see the compassion Marina has for them, since she herself has always had a weight problem rooted in her upbringing. These are deep-seated issues that she battles every moment of every day.

Being able to forgive oneself, and others, is a primary and necessary component of compassion.

Living In The Ju

Compassion is the highest level of humanity, which we in the Buddhist arts, Taoist arts and all religions strive for. Unfortunately, it is also one of the hardest levels to achieve.

As a student progresses through the Kata, techniques begin to soften. I believe students should also focus on their compassion. It may actually be a much harder thing to do than making your blocks more circular and fluid, or opening the palm to allow the energy to flow. In the midst of conflict, we naturally tense our fists and take a rigid stance with our emotions flying uncontrollably. It is a natural reaction to stress.

We have all been slighted one way or another in our lives. People do horrible things to one another. The reasons vary tremendously and everyone can usually justify it one way or another. It leaves us scratching our heads because it never makes any sense. We even do it to ourselves through self-sabotage. It's called, "The Human Condition": We do what we do just because we are human. I know I have been in that position as both giver and taker. I also know the power that forgiveness has and the destructive force that withholding it creates.

In my training, I constantly remind myself to soften up, to relax, to *let go* of my tension, and lately, this also pertains to my emotions. I have felt the warmth of compassion in my technique. I strive to embed it deeply into my Kata. It feels good and I embrace it in my teaching. I think this is what Master Toguchi meant when he wrote, "teach your juniors kindly", which brings me to the Ju in GoJu-Ryu.

There seems to be a strong connection between compassion, forgiveness and the Ju side of the art.

We are brothers and sisters in the Martial Arts, and we should always keep the Ju in our hearts when we train. If someone does wrong to you, try hard to forgive them and learn from it. Then move on past it or else you risk becoming like others in the art who have moved into the dark places, destroying all in their paths, as well as themselves.

Chapter 8: The Peace Within

Facing Your Worst Enemy

Can you face your worst enemy? Do you even know who it is? I have shocking news for you. *It is you.*

The hardest thing anyone could do is take a hard, critical look at themselves and change what they do not like. Most of us resist seeing ourselves as the outside world sees us. Studying the Martial Arts has shown me one thing very clearly: If I cannot see myself for who I truly am, then I cannot see others for who they truly are. My perceptions will always be colored by the filters I have put over my own eyes.

As a student of the art, it is my responsibility to remove those filters and look into my soul. Who am I? What do I believe in? Do I trust *me*? In order to put my head down on my pillow at night and sleep peacefully, I need to answer those questions. I need to make me right with *me*, before I can be right for someone else.

As far as GoJu is concerned, the Go is looking out, and the Ju is looking in, beneath the surface, and facing who you really are. If you don't like what you see, change it. That is what Kata is all about – working on yourself to change who you are, how you see things, how you do things, how you treat others – from the inside out, little by little.

Face it, we've all hurt others and self-sabotaged at one point or another in life. No one is without fault or sin. Who we are is the most important thing in life.

The stepping stones of Kata help us decipher our lives. Through the process of learning, practicing and working hard to perfect our Kata we discover our true selves and develop the tools to become an enlightened being; one who projects compassion outward without fear to help make this world a better place. It is hard work indeed; in fact at times it is bitter work. And that is what Kung Fu actually means, "Bitter work".

I've worked very hard to become who I am today, and when I look back at my life and see what Karate has done for me – I like what I see.

Epilogue

I gave a late draft of this book to my son Tyler to work on the graphic design. He is an eclectic person having talents in many areas and he is a very creative thinker. After reading the book, I asked him what his "take away" was. He said, "Dad, that 'circle of shoes' Uncle Robert put you in when you were a kid… it was a Mandala, and you were the center of it!"

This book has been dedicated to those who have

gone before

and transmitted their knowledge

faithfully and fully.

I bow and say:

"**THANK YOU VERY MUCH**"

Appendix

Mindfulness Or Mindlessness

A new buzzword in psychology today is "mindfulness". Mindfulness meditation is being taught at businesses, schools, special seminars and in psychologist's private practice. It is derived from Zen Buddhism and aims to create a way of life revolving around "loving kindness". Mindfulness training helps people in times of stress. It is said that *depression* is living in the past and *worrying* is living in the future. Mindfulness training keeps us in the *present* and is a way of calming oneself. When one is mindful, all thoughts are present, yet none is given any special weight. You become an observer of thoughts, as if they were clouds passing overhead. Mindfulness requires a certain amount of non-attachment. As thoughts occur naturally, you just let them go.

Mindlessness, on the other hand, is not paying attention to anything. In other words; not thinking things through, and not having any kind of awareness of what is happening at any given time. You act on instinct only. It is a lower form of thinking and can get you in a lot of trouble, maimed or even killed.

Meditation

There are many forms of meditation. Meditation calms the nerves and improves clear thinking. Meditation helps rejuvenate the mind, body and spirit. Meditation, for the Martial Artist, is a requirement if you want to reach Mushin and the higher spiritual planes.

The following are several effective methods of meditation:

Mindfulness: While seated comfortably, mindfulness-breathing focuses on the "out breath". Breathe in, then out. As you reach the end of the out breath, release all of the thoughts and feelings you have. The "in breath" is not a point of focus because the in breath happens naturally. As thoughts materialize, watch them float by as if they were clouds passing over a mountain. All breathing is through the nose.

Transcendental Meditation: Seated meditation, concentrating on a single-syllable word (Mantra) for 20 minutes, two times a day. If you notice you are thinking any thoughts, go back to your Mantra. Breathe slowly and calmly through your nose.

Sitting Breathe: Sit in a chair, feet flat on ground, palms down on your lap. Breathe in through your nose slowly pressing the tip of your tongue against the roof of your mouth for eight counts, hold for eight counts, drop your tongue and exhale out the mouth for eight counts, and hold for eight counts. As you repeat this breathing pattern, you should start sweating profusely after a few minutes. Repeat this breathing for up to 20 minutes, twice a day. It is a powerful method and will help you to generate Chi.

Clearing Space: This is my favorite. Close your eyes and breathe in through your nose as deeply as you can, into your Dantian. Feel the breath filling your entire body, expanding it. Then imagine the breath expanding past your body, as a mist filling the room. Try to feel the mist pushing up against the walls of the room, taking into account the size and shape of the room. Then, if there are other people in the room, sense their energies and allow them to become one with your breath. Release any negative energy enveloped in the mist by passing it through you, purified as you breath out of your mouth. Repeat for as long as you like.

Sanchin: Sanchin Kata is considered *moving* meditation, as compared to the aforementioned sitting meditations. Sanchin is a powerful meditation, incorporating very slow movements, executed with intense twisting dynamic tension and slow deep breathing into the Dantian.

It takes many years to perfect Sanchin and be able to enter into a deep state of mindfulness meditation while generating and manipulating lively and vibrant Chi.

Sanchin also incorporates the basic fighting concepts and principles of GoJu-Ryu. It is said that Karate starts with Sanchin and ends with Sanchin. You need a qualified, hands-on teacher to learn Sanchin Kata properly. If you do Sanchin incorrectly you may damage yourself. Sanchin is a very powerful meditation.

Special Thanks

Marina Kamen: Mrs. Kamen is a Grammy-nominated and Billboard-charting recording artist, as well as a composer, producer, director, commercial casting director, choreographer, certified fitness professional and mother of three. She has written and recorded over 450 original songs and produced commercials for television and radio for over 30 years. Mrs. Kamen's original music catalogue, fitness video workout programs and podcast series can be found at HighEnergyFitness.com.

Kow Loon Ong: Founder, Chairman and Chief Instructor of the Chi-I-Do Karate Do organization. Mr. Ong has practiced and taught the Martial Arts for over 50 years and has branch Dojos in Trinidad, Puerto Rico and throughout the United States. Mr. Ong is a master of Traditional Okinawan GoJu-Ryu, Matayoshi Kingai-Ryu and Kobudo. Mr. Ong studied with Seikichi Toguchi, Shinpo Matayoshi, Peter Urban, Shoichi Yamamoto, Akira Kawakami and Zen Priest Reverend Sogen Sakiyama. Kayo currently teaches Martial Arts in the New York City Public School system and at the Chi-I-Do Headquarters in Chinatown, NYC. Chi-I-Do.net

Gary Gabelhouse: Gary Gabelhouse is a published author, world explorer and longtime student of Asian Martial Arts. He continues to train and teach Daitoryu Aikijujitsu and Traditional Okinawan GoJu-Ryu Karate. Gabelhouse.com. Gary's writings and published books including his study of Mudra, Mantra and Mandala

Melvin Isidore Morgenstein, Ed.D. Columbia University Graduate School – Full Professor Emeritus.

Robert Mark Kamen, Ph.D. Screenwriter, Martial artist, and creator of The Karate Kid. KamenWines.com

Image Credits

Graphic Design by: Tyler Kamen
Cover art by: Erika Pochybova and James W. Johnson

Image Credits: "Map Of China pg. 6 in Public Domain • "Kanryo Higashionna" pg. 9 in Public Domain • "Chojun Miyagi" pg. 10 in Public Domain • "Seiko Higa" pg. 12 in Public Domain • "Seikichi Toguchi" pg. 13 in Public Domain • "Seed" pg. 18 in Public Domain • "Circle of Shoes" pg. 20 © Dmytro Zinkevych/123rf.com • "Kayo Killed My Karate" pg. 26 © Roy Kenneth Kamen • "Kow Loon Ong Head" pg.28 © Roy Kenneth Kamen • "Kow Loon Ong Crane" pg.28 © Kow Loon Ong • "Walkin The Path" pg 34 in Public Domain • "Yin / Yang" pg. 50 in Public Domain • Change Clock" pg. 52 in Public Domain • "Karate Kid" pg. 56 © Roy Kenneth Kamen • "Great Oak Tree" pg. 57 © Roy Kenneth Kamen • "Building" pg. 59 © lightwise/123rf.com • "Mandala" pg. 64 in Public Domain • "Open Hand" pg. 68 in Public Domain • "Upraised Hand in Prayer pg. 81 © hikrcn /123rf.com • "Stepping Stones" pg. 83 © lightwise /123rf.com • "Holding Yin-Yang" pg. 86 in Public Domain • "Sanchin Mandala" pg. 90 in Public Domain • "Tensho Mandala" pg. 92 © sacred-geometry.com • "Saifa Mandala" pg. 94 © Peter Barreda • "Seiyunchin Mandala" pg. 96 © Paul Heussenstamm • "Seisan Mandala" pg. 98 © Piper Lane • "Sepai Mandala" pg. 100 © Rebecca Wang • "Shisochin Mandala" pg. 102 © Steve Dubois • "Sanseiru Mandala pg. 104 © Nestaman • "Kururunfa Mandala" pg. 106 sacred-geometry.com • "Peichurin Mandala" pg. 108 © Bram Janssens/123rf.com • "Grand Buddha" pg. 109 © Thanawat Wongsuwannathorn/123rf.com • "Prayer Hands" pg. 112 in Public Domain • "Earth Globe" pg. 122 in Public Domain • "Standing Buddha" pg. 124 © aoo3771/123rf.com • "Before & After" pg. 133 © Roy Kenneth Kamen • "Toguchi & Kamen" pg. 141 © Roy Kenneth Kamen • "Kayo, Marina & Kamen" pg. 141 © Roy Kenneth Kamen

Grand Master Seikichi Toguchi with Roy Kenneth Kamen
1982

Kow Loon Ong (Kayo), Marina and Roy Kenneth Kamen
2015

About The Author

Roy Kenneth Kamen has studied Karate since 1965. He earned his second degree black belt in Traditional Okinawan GoJu-Ryu Karate and a first degree black belt in Okinawan Kobudo from Master Seikichi Toguchi, a first-generation student of the founder of GoJu-Ryu, Grand Master Chojun Miyagi, in 1980. Mr. Kamen currently holds an eighth-degree black belt and trains with Chi-I-Do International in New York City.

Mr. Kamen owns and operates Kamen Entertainment Group, Inc., a New York City based Entertainment Production company with his wife and partner Marina Kamen since 1987. Kamen Entertainment Group has won over 140 top industry awards and produced over 30,000 radio, television, movie, music and live theater productions. Clients include: Verizon, American Express, Mercedes, Jet Blue, Kelloggs, Disney, Hasbro, AT&T, Sony, Priceline, Lancome. Kamen.com.

Mr. and Mrs. Kamen have been married for over 34 years and have three grown and successful children, all living and working in New York City.

KARATE:

BENEATH THE SURFACE

BY: ROY KENNETH KAMEN

www.ingramcontent.com/pod-product-compliance
Lightning Source LLC
Chambersburg PA
CBHW070621300426
44113CB00010B/1614